Elon Musk Biography

By

Phillip G. Harris

© Copyright 2017 by Phillip G. Harris- All rights reserved.

This document is geared towards providing exact and reliable information in regards to the topic and issue covered. The publication is sold on the idea that the publisher is not required to render an accounting, officially permitted, or otherwise, qualified services. If advice is necessary, legal or professional, a practiced individual in the profession should be ordered.

- From a Declaration of Principles which was accepted and approved equally by a Committee of the American Bar Association and a Committee of Publishers and Associations.

In no way is it legal to reproduce, duplicate, or transmit any part of this document by either electronic means or in printed format. Recording of this publication is strictly prohibited, and any storage of this document is not allowed unless with written permission from the publisher. All rights reserved.

The information provided herein is stated to be truthful and consistent, in that any liability, in terms of inattention or otherwise, by any usage or abuse of any policies, processes, or directions contained within is the solitary and utter responsibility of the recipient reader. Under no circumstances will any legal responsibility or blame be held against the publisher for any reparation, damages, or monetary loss due to the information herein, either directly or indirectly.

Respective authors own all copyrights not held by the publisher.

The information herein is offered for informational purposes solely and is universal as so. The presentation of the information is without a contract or any type of guarantee assurance.

The trademarks that are used are without any consent, and the publication of the trademark is without permission or backing by the trademark owner. All trademarks and brands within this book are for clarifying purposes only and are owned by the owners themselves, not affiliated with this document.

To my wife and beautiful two daughters.

And to every man and woman who is pursuing a dream.

"I think that's the single best piece of advice: constantly think about how you could be doing things better and questioning yourself." – Elon Musk

Table of Contents

Chapter 1: Introduction.................................6
Chapter 2: Early Life in South Africa 9
Chapter 3: Move to North America 18
Chapter 4: Internet Pioneer........................24
Chapter 5: SpaceX 32
Chapter 6: Tesla Motors 47
Chapter 7: Technological Innovations 65
Chapter 8 – His Greatest Inspirations 77
Chapter 9 – How can he Inspire us? 94
Chapter 10 – Personal Life 99
Chapter 11: Private Thoughts 115
Chapter 12: An Uncertain Future 121
Chapter 13: Conclusion..............................127
30 Lesser Known Facts.............................. 129
Top 15 Quotes 134
Bibliography 140

Chapter 1: Introduction

Elon Musk is an engineer, inventor, software engineer, and businessman extraordinaire. He was born in South Africa to a Canadian mother and a South African father of British and American descent. At the age of 17, he moved to Canada, and shortly after that to the United States, obtaining his American citizenship in the early 2000s. He had an active role in the development and evolution of PayPal and is the CEO of rocket company SpaceX and electric car manufacturer Tesla Motors.

He is also associated with the SolarCity solar panel company and OpenAI, a new business dedicated to keeping artificial intelligence from becoming a hazard to humanity. As of April 2016, he has an estimated net worth of around $12.3 billion, making him the 68th wealthiest person in the United States.

From the time he was a child, Musk had an uncompromising dedication and an extraordinary intelligence. He taught himself computer programming at the age of 10, programming and selling his first video game when he was 12. He was one of the early entrepreneurs in Silicon Valley, moving there at the age of 24 in 1995 to begin an internet business directory called Zip2; the sale of this site in the late '90s was the first step in establishing his vast fortune and paved the way for his future business ventures.

Musk's goals for his various businesses are lofty: he aims to change the world and humanity's place in it. He plans to accomplish this by reducing global warming through his sustainable energy efforts, like Tesla Motors and SolarCity, and also to lessen the threat of human extinction by making it possible to colonize Mars. This last goal drives most of his other business ventures in some way or another but is most evident in his company SpaceX, which designs and builds rocket engines and spacecraft, and is one of two companies currently under contract with NASA to develop spacecraft rated for human travel.

Musk's work in his various companies has earned him a plethora of awards and accolades. In 2007, he was named *R&D Magazine's* Innovator of the Year and *Inc Magazine's* Entrepreneur of the Year, and won an Index Design award for his work on the Tesla Roadster. His work on the Falcon 1 launch vehicle won him accolades from the American Institute of Aeronautics and Astronautics in 2007-08.

The National Wildlife Federation gave him the National Conservation Achievement Award in 2008 for his work with Tesla Motors and SolarCity. In 2010, *Time Magazine* named him one of the 100 people who most affected the world; in 2011, *Forbes* listed him as one of America's 20 Most Powerful CEOs under 40. In 2014, the World Technology Network gave him two of the 20 available World Technology Awards, one in each the Energy and Space categories.

Though he was not born in the United States, Musk describes himself as "nauseatingly pro-American," and has described the nation as "inarguably the greatest country that has ever existed on Earth." He has made significant political contributions to both Republicans and Democrats. He believes in using the political system to advance technology and better the human race and has lobbied for the government to establish a carbon tax on gas-guzzling vehicles and companies to help limit the effects of global warming on the environment.

Though he has gotten some flack for contributing to PACs that are considered to be anti-environment or anti-science, Musk is unique among entrepreneurs in that he often seems to care more about his ideological goals than his profit margin.

Regardless of how one feels about his political contributions, there is no denying that he has single-handedly advanced human development, especially in the area of space exploration, through his continuing work and innovation.

Chapter 2: Early Life in South Africa

Elon Reeve Musk was born in Pretoria, South Africa on June 28, 1971. Though born in Africa, his ancestry was mostly derived from North America—Canadian on his mother's side, while his father's ancestors were born in Minnesota; he also had British and Pennsylvania Dutch ancestry.

There were also many entrepreneurs in the Musk family line; an inner drive for business is one of the many things Elon could be said to have inherited. Musk's first and middle names both came from relatives on his mother's side: Elon from his maternal great-grandfather (John Elon Haldeman), while Reeve was a title that means President or leader, held by his maternal step great-grandfather, who was Reeve of Excelsior Municipality in Saskatchewan, Canada.

Musk's parents were both entrepreneurs themselves. His Mother, Maye Haldeman, worked as a model as a young woman in Canada, and though she continued to model throughout her life—even well into her sixties—she set up her practice as a nutritionist and dietician after moving to South Africa.

His father, Errol, was an electromechanical engineer and an astute business person. Maye Musk described Errol as a "relentless suitor" when they met in university, proposing to her multiple times over the course of seven years before she finally relented and agreed to wed him. As might be expected, their marriage was complicated from the start. Elon was their oldest child, conceived on the couple's honeymoon and he was born nine months and two days after their wedding date. His two siblings were born in quick succession—his brother Kimbal came along in 1972, and his sister Tosca in 1974.

For the first nine years of his life, Musk's family lived in Waterkloof, an upscale suburb of Pretoria. The family owned one of the largest homes in Pretoria thanks to Errol's success in his engineering business, and the children had a full staff of help to take care of them. In 1980, however, his parents divorced, his mother moving to the family's holiday home in Durban, South Africa, on the eastern coast. The three children initially moved with their mother, but shortly after that decided to go back to Pretoria with his father.

Elon has later stated, "My father seemed sad and lonely, and my mom had three kids, and he did not have any. It seemed unfair." Possibly, considering Elon's already budding interest in business and computers, there was a certain selfish motivation to learn more about these topics of interest, as well.

Even from a very young age, Musk showed an incredible intelligence and drive. His mother Maye had said that he understood things more quickly than other children, even when he was very young, but also had a tendency to fall into a trance from which no one could rouse him. These moments happened so often and lasted so long his parents started to fear that he was deaf. Maye described it as going "into his brain" and him being in "another world," a habit he has to this day, though his family has learned to ignore it.

He also had a tendency to wander off and be drawn toward the things that interested him. Maye remembered multiple times she'd be walking around with the three children and would realize Elon was missing. She would often find him sitting on the floor of a bookstore, happily devouring some text that seemed far too advanced for his age. His mother remembers him reading the entire Encyclopedia Britannica around age eight—and remembering most of what he read.

Musk himself tells a story of when he was six as an example of his uniqueness as a child and his early dedication. There was one point when his mom grounded him and wouldn't allow him to accompany the family to a cousin's party. Elon thought the reason he'd been grounded was unjust. Rather than argue with his mother, though, he waited until they left to the party—then walked there himself to join them, some seven miles away through Pretoria. Elon arrived at the party just as his family was walking out to leave.

His mother, understandably, panicked. This is just one poignant example of young Elon's precociousness. His sister, Tosca, has also said he was honest to a fault and extremely blunt, even as a child. However, she's quick to point out that the intention is not to be mean; he simply sees things in a logical way, and considers honesty to be necessary—and did even as a child. These early traits would show again over and over throughout Elon Musk's life, eventually transforming into exactly the qualities that make a successful business person.

Life with Errol Musk

Elon's father Errol was born in 1946 in South Africa to parents of North American and British descent. He was described as an astute engineer with a bit of a swashbuckling edge; his engineering consulting practice made him very wealthy as a young man, and by the time Elon came to live with him after the divorce, Errol was in his mid-thirties and already semi-retired. Friends and family describe Errol as a "serial entrepreneur," a trait Elon undeniably acquired from his father. Among Errol's projects as a mechanical and electrical engineer were large-scale endeavors like office buildings, residential subdivisions, retail complexes, and even an air force base.

Always a diversified businessman, Errol also owned part of an emerald mine in Zambia and would take his sons to see it from a young age. This was not unusual for the family; Errol frequently traveled for work and often took his children along with him to see what he did and learn from the experience.

Errol did not want his children to grow up as rich children often do, not understanding the value of hard work or believing that everything in life should be handed to them. He was big in both education and life experiences as shaping a person's future. During Elon's childhood, he would sometimes lecture the boy for hours at a time, giving him college-level knowledge when he was not yet even in high school. Errol seemed to delight in being hard on his children, rarely allowing them to engage in the typical childhood diversions (and removing much of the fun from the ones he did allow).

Both Elon and Kimbal describe a game Errol would have them play called "America America." This "game" involved Errol sending the housekeepers away for the day and instead having Elon and Kimbal do the chores, in the way Errol said children had to do over in the United States.

In addition to taking his children on trips to the distant places Errol visited for his work, he would bring them along to his every day worksites, as well. Both Elon and his younger brother Kimbal were required to join Errol occasionally at his engineering jobs. They learned the physical aspects of an engineer's work at these sites—they would lay bricks, install plumbing, or wire the electrical systems alongside their father, in this way gaining an early understanding of how things are built and how they work.

Elon described his father as an exceptionally talented engineer who "knew how every physical object worked." Errol considered it one of his missions as a father to ensure that his children gained that same understanding.

On the other side of this job ethic, Errol instilled in his children was his often cold and authoritative nature. He was an intense man throughout his life, always very present in the world and with a force about him that made it clear to others. All of Errol's children have stayed relatively mute regarding the details of their upbringing with their father; reading between the lines, one gets the sense of something profoundly awful that happened during their young years at home.

At times, these difficulties sound akin to a kind of psychological torture. Maye has since said about Errol that he was not friendly to anyone, and few people got along with him, but also wouldn't share details, only saying, "I do not want to tell stories because they are horrendous." Kimbal also speaks only vaguely of his father, stating just that "he has serious chemical stuff" and describing his upbringing as "emotionally challenging," though he acknowledges these challenges no doubt made both brothers into the successful men they are today. Elon has been similarly vague where his father is concerned.

He describes his childhood as one with many happy things in it, one that was rich with good opportunities, but not as a childhood that could be overall described as happy. Reading between the lines, it is very clear that his father's personality had a lot to do with robbing the joy from Elon's childhood—a task that seems nearly impossible, considering the wealth and adventure the Musk children were able to enjoy.

Developing interest in programming

The first computers went on sale in South Africa in 1980, when Elon Musk was around nine years old. He saw his first computer at the Sandton City Mall in Johannesburg when he was ten years old and instantly knew he had to have it. The electronics store that stocked the computers was typically more interested in selling sound equipment and had only one small corner stocked with the new device, but Musk was enthralled by this idea of a machine that could be made to think and hounded his father to buy him one. Soon enough, Elon was the proud owner of a Commodore VIC-20. This early computer came with five kilobytes of memory and included a workbook to learn the programming language BASIC.

The workbook was supposed to be completed over the course of several months by the adults who were intended to buy and use the computer. Elon remembers, "I just got super OCD on it and stayed up for like three days with no sleep and did the entire thing." This new programming language enchanted him just as much as the computer itself had; he described it as "the most super-compelling thing" that he had ever seen.

Though Errol bought Elon his computer, he was not bitten by the same technology bug as his son. Though he was an engineer, he was more interested in the physical, hands-on aspects of the construction than the technological possibilities. It is accurate to describe Errol Musk as something of a Luddite, generally distrustful of—or at best, indifferent to—the newest technologies. When he bought Elon the computer, he had the opinion the device was only good for playing games, not something that one could use to perform real engineering.

For Elon, though, the computer was far more than a collection of parts aimed at providing a few hours of digitized diversion. Though he was close to his family throughout his life, Elon never developed a strong relationship with the other children in his neighborhood or school—quite the opposite, in fact; Elon suffered from bullying throughout his childhood. The computer provided a refuge from the violence of the real world, a place where things could be made to happen the way he wanted them—and a place where things made sense.

Errol had said of his son that "he loved computer science before anyone even knew what it was in South Africa." By the time Elon was a preteen, he'd already mastered the BASIC language and was starting to gain recognition for his programming prowess. In 1984, at the age of 12, Musk programmed a video game called *Blastar* using his coding skills. It was a simple arcade-style game similar to others being played at the time. The player has a ship, which can be moved up and down or side to side, and shoots at lighted dot "enemies" that came down from the top of the screen to earn points.

Simple though it may seem to modern gamers, this was on the same level as the games most adults were programming during the 1980s. Elon sold his game to a magazine called *PC and Office Technology* for $500, which he then—in true Musk fashion—invested in pharmaceutical stocks. The money won from this video game eventually grew into the funds he would use to buy his plane ticket to Canada as a late teen. *Blastar*, meanwhile, is still available on the internet as an HTML game.

School life

Elon Musk started his education at Waterkloof House Preparatory Academy in his suburb of Pretoria. The culture in the education system of South Africa during the 1970s and 1980s was not one most would see today as a healthy environment to encourage children to learn. Bullying was so rampant it was considered simply part of the education.

Newcomers to the school were expected to fight the school's top thug as a rite of passage. Errol describes the environment as a place where "hatred was endemic," saying that "no one fought fair" and it was common for groups of boys to gang up on their victims and even use blunt objects as weapons to further enhance their bullying. Kimbal remembers it being "a rough culture…kids gave Elon a very hard time, and it had a huge impact on his life." His sister Tosca remembers that children had no recourse. "In South Africa, if you are getting bullied, you still have to go to school," she said.

It is perhaps no surprise that a smart, precocious, and somewhat odd child like Elon Musk would be a frequent target for bullies. Despite his intellectual prowess, his emotional and social intelligence did not develop quite as quickly. He would be blunt and honest with the other children, as was his nature—a habit that didn't earn him many friends.

What was worse, he would correct the factual errors of the other schoolmates, a habit he thought of as being helpful, but that was perceived by his fellow students as arrogant, alienating him further.

The bullying Elon suffered at the hands of his classmates was close to constant, but it culminated in a particularly brutal incident when he was around 12 years old. A group of boys threw him down a flight of steps and beat him until he passed out. As a result of this incident, Elon was hospitalized for two weeks; it left him with a jagged septum that never healed correctly and had to be surgically corrected later on in his adulthood.

The beating was bad enough Errol said he hardly recognized his child when he came to see him at the hospital. Errol attempted to file charges with the Randburg police department, but they were so accustomed to the culture of bullying that they dismissed the incident as "skoolseuns wat rondspeel" (schoolboy hijinks) and never took it any further.

The only recourse left to Errol to help his son avoid his bullies was to transfer him to another school, which he did, pulling Elon out of the Waterkloof House Preparatory system and instead enrolling him at Pretoria Boys High School. The environment here was slightly better for Elon, who was at least never put back into the hospital by his classmates.

Following his move to his new school, Elon went through a period he later referred to as his "existential crisis." He became very interested in the philosophical writings of nihilists like Nietzsche and Schopenhauer. On the flip side of this, he also became very interested in the humorous science fiction of writers like Douglass Adams, devouring *The Hitchhikers Guide to the Galaxy* in his mid-teens. From this, he gained the insight that "if you ask the right questions, the answers are easy—the hard part is asking the right questions." This seemingly bizarre mix of ideologies absorbed in his teen years would go on to inform the remainder of his adult life.

It was while he was attending Pretoria Boys High School that Elon made his first attempt at being an entrepreneur. At the age of 16, he attempted to open a video arcade near his school with the help of his brother. They got the lease on the building, arranged suppliers, and had everything in place, but couldn't get permission to open from the city and were forced to abandon the project.

It was around this same time that Elon started to become truly interested in moving to North America. He tried to convince his father to move to the United States, and at one point seemed to have convinced him to do so, but his father reneged at the last minute. Elon was frustrated by what he saw as the restrictions being put in his future if he were to remain in South Africa and decided to take matters into his hands. Using the money he'd made from his video game as a child, Elon purchased a plane ticket and relocated, on his own, to Canada.

Chapter 3: Move to North America

Throughout his teens, Elon Musk wanted to move to the United States. He saw it as the place where the future was happening; Silicon Valley was his version of the Promised Land. As Musk said, "Whenever I'd read about cool technology it would tend to be in the United States, or more broadly, North America." His father was unwilling to move to the United States, however, being too firmly established in his career and life in South Africa.

Elon tried to get US citizenship but couldn't at the time. Never one to give up easily, Elon looked for a workaround that would at least get him to the continent where the cutting edge technology was being developed.

Elon was also eager to leave South Africa for other reasons. Between his father's intense and sometimes cruel manner and the regular beatings he'd received during his childhood education, it is no wonder he'd want to leave the landscape behind. Aside from this, the political situation in South Africa at the time was one Elon wanted to get away from.

He did not support apartheid and was unwilling to stay in a country that continued to practice it. In other words, though getting to the United States was the ultimate goal, Elon was also eager to escape to just about anywhere else.

Even though she'd been living in South Africa for years, Elon's mother Maye—having been born in Regina, Saskatchewan—was still a Canadian citizen. This ultimately proved Elon's gateway to the west. As the son of a Canadian citizen, Elon was able to obtain a Canadian passport for himself.

Within three weeks of receiving the document, he was on a plane to North America.

Ontario

Though he'd managed to get closer to the geographical place he wanted to be, Elon's journey was far from over. Despite Errol Musk's vast wealth, he was unwilling to give Elon money for his college education unless his son remained in South Africa. It is unclear what his motivation was for this decision—whether he simply wanted to keep his family close together or whether it was a further attempt to make Elon grow through adversity.

Even though he was still in his teens, Elon had some savings of his own—the returns on the $500 worth of stock he'd purchased with his *Blastar* money. This money was enough to get him to Canada but hardly enough to live on. He arrived in Ontario in June of 1989, just before his 18th birthday, with little money and no definite plans for how he would make more.

Maye Musk still had family in Canada. Before leaving South Africa, he'd heard from his mother of a great-uncle living in Montreal and planned to hook up with this uncle once he landed. Maye had sent a letter to this uncle before Elon left for his trip, but ever impatient to get on with his future; Elon left the country before a reply came in.

The reply had arrived while he was in transit, though, and it brought bad news: said great-uncle had relocated to Minnesota, and Musk had nowhere to stay. He temporarily checked into a youth hostel in Montreal while he figured out his next step.

There were others of his mother's relatives in Canada, of course, and Elon made the decision to track them down. He bought a bus ticket to Saskatchewan, stopping in the small town of Swift Current where a second cousin of Musk was living.

This cousin was still in Canada and invited Elon to stay with him on the farm. While living there, Musk did whatever odd jobs he could to earn some cash. He tended his cousin's vegetable garden and shoveled out his grain bins. He went briefly to Vancouver, where he learned to cut logs with a chainsaw.

He even briefly took a job cleaning the boiler room of a lumber mill. It was uncomfortable and dangerous work, but it paid $18 per hour—enough to start building a new savings account. Elon traveled western Canada taking on these odd jobs for about a year before he finally had enough to consider college.

Elon's brother Kimbal joined him in Canada in the fall of 1990, the same semester Elon enrolled at Queen's University in Kingston, Ontario, at the age of 19. Where Elon was a somewhat awkward, nerdy genius, Kimbal was affable and good with people; this combination made them virtually unstoppable when they worked together. They started major cold-calling players in the Canadian economy and asking for lunch meetings.

This was how they met Peter Nicholson, a top executive at the Bank of Nova Scotia who would end up becoming one of Elon's most trusted advisors. After their conversation, Nicholson offered Elon a summer internship at the bank.

His time at Queen's University did more for Elon's personal development than it did for his intellectual abilities, which were already well beyond most of his classmates. He met people whom he felt he could relate to, people who respected his ambition and genius, and through them was able to become friendlier and lose the know-it-all attitude he'd had in younger years. Ever the entrepreneur, Elon started selling PCs and computer parts out of his dorm room to make some extra cash. He met many people at Queens University who would remain his friends and colleagues for life, including his first wife, Justine Wilson. However, Canada had never been Elon's intended destination.

Two years into his degree, Elon received a scholarship from the University of Pennsylvania. The scholarship did not cover his entire tuition—he would graduate with a significant student loan debt—but it was his legal entry point to the United States. In 1992, he finally arrived in America.

Pennsylvania

By the time he reached the University of Pennsylvania, Elon Musk had matured out of some of his schoolboy awkwardness and had learned to channel his intensity into his work. He pursued dual degrees from U Penn: an economics degree from the Wharton School and a Bachelor of Science in physics from the College of Arts and Sciences. The physics program at U Penn finally introduced Musk to other people who thought as he did—in other words, he located the other nerds; he had finally found his tribe.

One of these fellow nerds was Adeo Ressi, who was Musk's roommate during his time at U Penn. Like Kimbal, Ressi served as a colorful and jovial foil to Musk's more reserved attitude. After living together for a semester in the freshman dorm, the pair rented a ten-bedroom house off-campus—a frat house that had previously been abandoned, allowing them to get it for relatively cheap. During the week, it was a place for quiet study; on the weekends, Ressi transformed it into an unofficial nightclub. Ressi describes it as "a full-out, unlicensed speakeasy." They'd charge five dollar admission then provide beer and Jell-O shots to the attendees. Musk, who did not like the taste of alcohol, would manage the money while the other students partied.

The ideas for many of the companies Musk would go on to found came out of his time at the University of Pennsylvania. In 1993, he wrote a paper for his economics degree that described a "Google-like" search engine, using link counting and PageRank technology; though he would not pursue this format, the ideas in it would help as he founded Zip2.

A December 1994 paper entitled "The Importance of Being Solar" outlined material improvements and solar plant construction ideas that he would later employ through his involvement in SolarCity. The most telling of his college papers, though, is one he wrote on ultracapacitors that outlined how it could revolutionize the construction of cars, planes, and rockets. These ideas, developed in his college years, would impact his work with both SpaceX and Tesla Motors.

California

In 1995, at the age of 24, Musk graduated from the University of Pennsylvania. He applied for—and was accepted into—the Ph.D. program at Stanford University, where he was supposed to begin work on an applied physics degree. He spent the summer between the end of his degree program at U Penn and the start of his Ph.D. program at Stanford writing business plans and internet software. Ressi, meanwhile, moved to New York and launched a city media website called "Total New York," one of the first advertiser-supported web media companies to be created. This idea inspired Musk and was lurking in the back of his mind when he moved to California.

As had been the case with his previous two colleges, enrolling at Stanford University was less about the studies, and more a means to an end. Musk had finally reached his "promised land" of Silicon Valley and, now that he was there, he was impatient to get on with his life. Musk lasted only two days in his Ph.D. program before dropping out. His brother Kimbal joined him in Palo Alto, where they rented an office for $400 a month that would also serve as their apartment.

The idea of internet commerce was relatively young but not completely new when the Musk brothers arrived in Silicon Valley. Amazon had just started in 1994; AOL was already underway, and in fact was the company that purchased Ressi's "Total New York" website in 1995. Starting an internet company in 1995 was impressive, and Musk certainly got in on the front edge of the trend, but it was perhaps not as innovative as Musk would imply in his later interviews.

In fact, this would be a common feature of Musk's companies throughout his life—not necessarily coming up with new ideas completely, but instead riffing off of other people's ideas in new ways that improve the concept or increase the profitability. By making minor improvements to existing concepts, Musk was able to make significant income without having to lay the groundwork for the new industry.

In the case of his first business in Silicon Valley, Musk riffed off of Ressi's "Total New York" concept, transferring it to California. He purchased a Yellow Pages CD Rom and then integrated it with mapping software to create a city listing website. This website would ultimately grow into Zip2, Elon Musk's first real business, and the first step in amassing his now-famous fortune.

Chapter 4: Internet Pioneer

Though they came from a family of great wealth, the Musk brothers in California had relatively limited means when they first got set up. Errol Musk gave them an investment of $28,000, which was enough to get their office space, buy licensing software, and obtain basic equipment. After that, though, the duo was essentially broke. Considering that Elon still had student loans to deal with from his time at the University of Pennsylvania, his lifestyle in these early years of entrepreneurship was hardly what you would expect from a future billionaire.

The Palo Alto office Musk had rented was incredibly affordable for a reason. It had a leaky ceiling and had been long abandoned. Kimbal and Elon had first to caulk the ceiling and replace the carpet before space could even really be used. For the first three months of their business venture, this office would serve as their home as well as their work space. They purchased a couple of futons to sleep on, had a small closet where they would keep their clothes, and would shower at the YMCA across the street.

Without a kitchen, they relied on cheap local restaurants for sustenance. Kimbal remembers, "Sometimes we ate four meals a day at Jack in the Box," a twenty-four-hour restaurant that suited the brothers' around the clock work schedule. Unable to afford a high-speed internet connection, Musk instead ran the program on his personal computer using an old-school dial-up modem, until an internet service provider on the floor below them in the building agreed to let Musk drill a hole in the floor and plug into their network. Though their life in this time was far from glamorous, these early years of Musk's career as an internet entrepreneur would go on to influence his business decisions throughout his life.

Zip2

Musk's first business was based on the city search guide he'd come up with upon moving to Silicon Valley. Though he'd matured as an individual during his time at Queen's University and the University of Pennsylvania, Elon Musk's strengths were still in the computer science arena—not necessarily his ability to interact with people. Luckily, Kimbal was the opposite: personable, affable, and an excellent salesman.

They quickly fell into a routine, where Musk would do all the coding of their service and handle all of the behind the scenes work while Kimbal would serve as their public face, even going so far as to make door-to-door sales of their new product.

The Yellow Pages information was a good start for Zip2's program, but Musk knew that to offer a truly unique and useful service that would make them competitive and profitable he needed to add more features to Zip2's program. He acquired a database that listed Bay Area businesses for relatively cheap. This database was relatively sparse regarding its information, giving little more than the business name and its address, but that was all Musk needed to get him to the next step.

With this information in their grasp, Musk contacted Navteq, an existing company that created digital maps and directions for early GPS navigation devices. When they contacted Navteq, the company gave the Musk brothers their technology free of charge—extremely good news, considering they were still struggling financially. Musk took this technology and merged it with his existing database then added extra maps to cover a range beyond the major metro area. He added custom turn by turn directions to the program and set it up to be visually appealing and easy to navigate on a home computer.

As the company grew, the Musk brothers added more staff on both sides of the operation. Shortly after starting, Kimbal had an entire team of salesmen to pitch their idea door to door. On the coding side, Elon hired a team of engineers to help him perfect their product. They also began to look for investors. One early investor was Greg Kouri, who would go on to help Musk co-found PayPal. In January of 1996, they also began to work with the venture capital firm Mohr Davidow. Their significant investment of around $3 million allowed the company to expand its focus beyond the Bay Area to the nation as a whole.

The investment of extra capital also allowed the brothers to transform their business model. Instead of simply selling door to door, they created a software package that they could sell to newspapers for the purpose of establishing local directories that could be aimed at either leisure activities—like restaurants and local attractions—or more practical things, like car dealerships or real estate agencies and offerings. Musk secured contracts with *The New York Times* and *The Chicago Tribune*, in addition to their local customers.

As positive as their work with Mohr Davidow was for the company from a profit and growth perspective, it had its downsides as well. The fact that they'd made such a major financial investment in Zip2 meant Mohr Davidow felt entitled to controlling the daily operations of the company, as well. A board of directors was established to help manage the quickly-growing company. Elon Musk wanted to become the company's CEO, but the new board members voted unanimously against it, believing him too young and inexperienced to successfully manage the company; he was instead relegated to a CTO role.

The title of CEO was instead given to Rich Sorkin, a former VP at the hardware manufacturer Creative Technology. Though he was a competent manager, Sorkin's vision for the company did not align perfectly with Musk's. Sorkin ended up soliciting investments from many of the same companies that were Zip2's customers, setting up an awkward situation in which they were doubly beholden to the needs of their consumers.

These early experiences with Zip2 would provide Musk with an invaluable lesson: he who controls the money controls the company. He quickly saw that allowing a single company to invest so much money in Zip2 had given them an inordinate amount of power over the operations and directions. Without their capital to match, Elon and Kimbal were relegated to minor figures within their own business. Musk spent the late '90s watching his company move in a direction he did not think was right, but was frustratingly powerless to do anything to change it.

In April of 1998, Sorkin started the process of selling Zip2 to CitySearch; Musk, who was tired of watching Sorkin squander his company's potential, did everything he could to fight against this move. He got the board of directors on his side and managed to spark a mutiny, getting Zip2's other managers to threaten to quit if Sorkin wasn't removed. This worked to stop the CitySearch merger and did get Sorkin removed from his position, but ultimately wasn't enough to save Zip2.

Derek Proudian, who worked for Mohr Davidow, was installed as CEO following Sorkin's departure. It is traditional wisdom that once a venture capitalist steps in as a company's CEO, that is the first death knell of the company and suggests a great number of disarrays at the corporate level. Zip2 was no exception to this rule. In February of 1999, less than a year after Proudian was named CEO, a deal was negotiated that would sell Zip2 to Compaq.

Musk was powerless to stop this deal from going forward. On the plus side, the sale of Zip2 was the largest sum paid to that point for an internet company. The total cash payment from Compaq was $307 million, along with $34 million in stock options. Of this, Elon received $22 million (around 7% of the overall sale) and Kimbal received $18 million.

Despite this windfall, Musk considered Zip2 to be a failure ultimately. His goal for the company had been to help build up the newly-created internet. Instead, he ended up just creating software that would be used by large, established companies. Zip2, meanwhile, was re-sold by Compaq—again for a tidy profit—and ended up dying in the bureaucracy of its new owners.

X.com

Not one to be deterred by failure and setbacks, Musk started designing his next company almost as soon as he'd received his payment for the sale of Zip2. Even if it hadn't lived up to Musk's original expectations, Zip2 had given him the financial stability to start a new company that would be completely under his control; though he would still need to secure investors to make the company succeed, he could have enough of his money involved in the company to keep these investors from seizing creative control. Musk invested $10 million of his Zip2 payment into his new company, which would be called X.com.

Musk's idea, this time, was to revolutionize the online financial services sector. Musk had seen that traditional banks were not inclined toward innovation and knew, if online commerce were to be revolutionized, it would have to be done by an outsider—and he felt he was in the perfect position to be that outsider, considering the business acumen and valuable lessons he'd gained from his experience with Zip2. During the summer of 1999, Musk secured an investment from Sequoia Capital, the same company that had backed such prominent organizations as Oracle, Cisco, and Apple. They gave Musk $25 million toward his new firm.

While his ambitions had been broad on the outside, over the course of X.com's development Musk scaled them back to a more manageable goal: to create a way to make payments through email. As was the theme throughout his career, Musk was not the only person—or even the first person—to have come up with this idea. A different company, Confinity, had already developed a similar product to the one Musk envisioned, which it called PayPal. Confinity had been founded in December 1998 by Max Levchin, Peter Thiel, Luke Nosek, and Ken Howery, primarily as a company to develop security software for handheld devices. They saw their PayPal service, which had only recently launched, as a minor aspect of their overall business plan; Elon Musk saw it as potentially the revolutionary payment method he'd envisioned when he started X.com.

In early 2000, less than a year after X.com was founded, Musk merged his company with Confinity. The combined venture kept the X.com name and decided to focus on the money transfer aspect of the business, a vision then-CEO Bill Harris did not share. Harris left the company in May of 2000; Elon Musk was all too eager to take over the position.

From the outset, Musk at the Confinity crew clashed, both regarding their ideologies and their personalities. In some ways, Musk became for Confinity what the Mohr Davidow executives had been for Zip2—sweeping in to change the very ideology of the company. Confinity founder Max Levchin would later say that working for Musk was very difficult. Musk had his very clear ideas of where he wanted this company to go, and though this implacability was likely in large part due to his lack of control over his previous company, it served to frustrate both Levchin and fellow founder Peter Thiel.

Musk's confidence in the future of the money transfer business led him to terminate the company's other online banking operations in October of 2000 so they could focus on further developing PayPal. He went on a two-week trip to meet with potential investors; during his absence, Levchin and Thiel orchestrated a coup, getting the board to fire Musk as CEO (ironically, in much the same way Musk had gotten Zip2 CEO Rich Sorkin removed). He came back to find that Thiel was the new CEO and that the company had been re-named to PayPal.

PayPal's early growth had been largely attributed to a viral marketing campaign, a relatively new concept for internet companies but a logical one considering the way the company operated. The idea was that when someone was sent money through PayPal, he or she would have to sign up for the service to retrieve it. However, this growth was not quite enough to bring in the kind of money it would take to develop the service further. In early 2002, PayPal's executive board decided to take the company public. Their IPO listed PayPal at $13 per share and generated $61 million in income for the company.

The PayPal sale

Though he'd been removed as CEO, Musk remained the largest shareholder in the PayPal company, holding around 11.7% of the shares. The coup orchestrated by Levchin and Thiel had wounded him emotionally, but Musk was a businessman first—and he had not been wounded enough to give up his financial stake in the company.

As with Zip2, Musk believed that PayPal had more potential to build up the internet than it was being used for. Being now outside the company's executive structure. However, Musk had no control or influence to make these opinions heard. The company's new executives did not share his interest in revolutionizing the internet banking industry. Instead, they were happy enough to turn the reins of the company over to a more established company in exchange for a financial windfall. In October of 2002, eBay acquired PayPal for $1.5 billion in stock.

Since Musk was still the primary shareholder, he received a significant portion of that money—around $165 million, not a bad payday considering he'd started X.com with only a $10 million investment.

As with Zip2, however, the financial benefit of the sale of PayPal was not enough to compensate for the negative feelings the entire experience had left Musk with. Even after the company was sold, he remarked that with 120 million customers using it and the high regard these customers had for the company—along with the trust factor that regards brought to the table—PayPal had "much-unleveraged value." It frustrated Musk to no end that, once again, a potentially revolutionary company had been reduced to a glorified feature to be used by other corporate entities through the process of sale and re-sale.

Though PayPal is still going strong (unlike Zip2), it certainly didn't change the world in the way Musk had envisioned when he founded X.com. Unlike most of Silicon Valley's internet entrepreneurs, Musk's ultimate goal was not just to make much money. He had far too much ambition for that.

Musk's first company had been taken over by venture capitalists and wrested out of his hands. His second company, he'd maintained financial control but, in merging with an established company, failed to establish or maintain ideological control, resulting in his ultimate removal. With an ever-growing fortune now at his disposal, Musk again set out to start a new business—and this time, he would succeed, through any means necessary, in providing the technological revolution he'd been aiming for since his arrival in Silicon Valley.

Chapter 5: SpaceX

SpaceX stands for "Space Exploration Technologies Corporation" and is one of Elon Musk's longest-running projects. Musk first started turning his gaze toward the stars when he thought about starting the Mars Oasis project in 2001. This project was intended to land a miniaturized greenhouse on the planet Mars. This greenhouse would grow crops of food in the Martian regolith—the layer of dust, soil, and broken rock that covers solid rock on terrestrial moons and planets. In the process of planning a potential trip to Mars, however, Musk realized that the travel would be, as he said, "prohibitively expensive," and that it would require a "fundamental breakthrough in rocket technology." Using his amassed fortune, Musk then set out to make that breakthrough.

The primary objective of SpaceX is to develop and manufacture launch vehicles for space travel. There are two broader goals at work: to advance rocket technology to the level that it will be possible to make a manned trip to Mars, and to regain the public's interest in space exploration, which Musk felt had waned at the start of the 21st century. The company is based in the Los Angeles suburb of Hawthorne, California, occupying a three-story facility that was originally built by the Northrop Corporation for the construction of Boeing 747 fuselages.

This building houses the offices, factory, and mission control of all of SpaceX's launches, though the rockets themselves are launched from various space facilities around the United States. Hawthorne has an incredible concentration of aerospace research labs and corporations. NASA's Jet Propulsion Laboratory is near the SpaceX facility, as are offices of Boeing, Lockheed Martin, Northrop Grumman, Raytheon, and BAE Systems. SpaceX also has regional offices scattered around the country, including Houston, Texas; Chantilly, Virginia; and Washington, DC.

In 2014, they opened a new office in Seattle, Washington, where a team of software developers and engineers is working on constructing a global satellite network. The immediate goal of this network is to bring the Internet to remote corners of the world, but like most of the projects SpaceX has undertaken, the ultimate purpose is related to Mars: this network would also allow communication with colonies established on the red planet.

SpaceX has sent several unmanned cargo shipments into space, both on commercial missions and through contracts with NASA, delivering supplies to the International Space Station. They currently use two orbital launch sites. Space Launch Complex 40 of the Cape Canaveral Air Force Station in Florida is used for launches using SpaceX's Falcon 9 launch vehicles, which send objects into low-Earth and geostationary orbits. Space Launch Complex 4 on Vandenberg Air Force Base (about 10 miles outside of Lompoc, California) is used for sending payloads to polar orbits and is the intended site of future launches using the Falcon Heavy launch vehicle.

The company has announced plans to add two more orbital launch facilities, with intended niches in mind for all of them, including one that will be designated as a commercial launch site, and one to be used for crewed missions. In addition to these facilities, they make use of two rocket test facilities: The Rocket Development and Test Facility in McGregor, Texas (which is owned by SpaceX) and a leased space at the Vertical Takeoff Vertical Landing test facility at Spaceport America in New Mexico.

As the largest private producer of rocket motors worldwide, SpaceX has developed three families of rocket engines: the

Merlin and Kestrel lines for launch vehicle propulsion, and the Draco RCS control thrusters. Two more designs are currently in development (the SuperDraco and the Raptor). They have produced more than 100 operational Merlin 1D engines, which currently holds the record for the industry's highest trust to weight ratio (155:1). A single Merlin 1D engine can deliver 650 kN of thrust, meaning it can lift about the equivalent of 40 cars. These engines are used in clusters to power the company's Falcon launch vehicles.

Since its founding in 2002, SpaceX has achieved numerous firsts in the industry. All three of its major vehicles (the Falcon 1, the Falcon 9, and the Dragon) were the first successful models of their kind to be built and launched by a privately-funded company.

SpaceX launched its first commercial delivery into geosynchronous orbit in 2013; it launched the Deep Space Climate Observatory in 2015, the company's first delivery beyond Earth's orbit. Its most recent concern has been to accomplish vertical landing of first stage rocketry on a solid platform, a mission they succeeded in for the first time on April 8, 2016, when a CRS-8 launch vehicle vertically landed on an ocean drone platform after having delivered a Dragon spacecraft into low-Earth orbit.

The business side of SpaceX

Like many of Elon Musk's businesses, SpaceX is revolutionary for its industry. It utilizes a high degree of vertical integration in the management of its supply chain, an unusual business strategy for the aerospace industry that has paid off in a huge way for the rocket company. The vertical integration was largely a by-product of Musk's feeling that none of the industry's current rocket manufacturers were making engines capable of accomplishing low-cost orbital launch. SpaceX builds and develops 85% of its vehicles in-house, including constructing its spacecraft, avionics, rocket engines, and rocket stages, and developing most of its software. Even so, the company has over 3,000 individual suppliers, around a third of which make deliveries on a weekly basis. The company both uses its rockets for launches and sells its rocket engines and parts to other aerospace companies (another way they are unusual in the industry).

SpaceX is funded privately, in no small part by Elon Musk himself, who has invested well over $100 million of his money. Its total funding in its first ten years of operation was around $1 billion, some of which came as part of their NASA contracts, some of which was invested by corporations and individuals. Though shares of SpaceX stock are not publically traded (with no plans to go public shortly) shares of stock have been purchased to raise funds. In January 2015, Musk received an additional $1 billion in funding from Google and Fidelity in exchange for 8.33% of the company. Though the records are no public, extrapolating from this data would put SpaceX's value at that point around $12 billion.

The company has expanded significantly over the course of its existence. In November of 2005, SpaceX had only 160 employees; by 2010, they reported 1,100; by 2015, nearly 5,000. Partially this is because of their expansion of operations, not only developing and making the launch vehicles and rocket engines but contracting with both government and private institutions to deliver payloads into space.

Though they only started launching vehicles in 2009, by late 2013 they had 50 launches under contract (two-thirds of which were for commercial customers). In 2014, they won 9 of the 20 orbital launch contracts available worldwide, stealing business from competitors like Arianespace's Ariane 5 and the

International Launch Services' Proton (in fact, it was the first year in a long while the Proton booked no commercial launches whatsoever).

In large part, SpaceX's growth and success can be contributed to their vertical integration. Building their rockets enables Musk's company to undercut its competitors—at only $6.5 million per launch in 2013, the Falcon 9 rockets were the cheapest in the industry. They can deliver shipments to orbit for only $2,500 per pound with the Falcon 9, and expect that price to drop to $1,000 per pound once they start using the Falcon Heavy. If they continue to find success with vertical landing, this will make their Falcon launch vehicles re-usable, lowering the costs even further. This undercutting has put pressure not only on other companies in the orbital launch business but other launch industries, like those for US military payloads.

Founding and early years

Following the multi-million dollar payout he'd received from the sale of PayPal, Musk wanted to invest his money, time, and energy into his long-held dream of space travel. He took his best friend from college (fellow entrepreneur Adeo Ressi) and an aerospace supplies expert (Jim Cantrell) on a trip to Moscow, Russia in October 2001, in the hopes of locating and purchasing used ICBM missiles that could be refurbished to send payloads into space. They met with several missile companies in Russia, including heavy-hitters NPO Lavochkin and Kosmotras. Since Musk's experience to this point had been exclusively in internet commerce—not in the aerospace industry—the Russian businessmen saw Musk as a novice and wouldn't take him seriously. Cantrell describes one of the Russian chief designers even spitting on Musk during a meeting. Ultimately, the group went back to the U.S. empty-handed.

Not one to give up easily, Musk returned to Russia a second time in February 2002, this time following a lead for three ICBMs he believed might be for sale. In addition to Ressi and Cantrell, Musk also brought along Mike Griffin, a former employee of NASA's Jet Propulsion Laboratory, in the hopes of lending their claim more credibility. They again met with Kosmotras, who this time at least extended them an offer: one ICBM for $8 million. When the company refused to negotiate, Musk left the meeting in a huff, seeing that cost as prohibitive for what he hoped to accomplish.

It was on the flight back from his second Russian expedition that Musk realized there was an alternative to buying overpriced used rockets: building them himself. He calculated that the raw materials involved in building a rocket represented only around 3% of their market value. If he applied the vertical integration and modular strategies he'd learned in his software engineering companies, he thought he could offer launch prices that were a tenth of what was currently on the market, while still maintaining a 70% profit margin on the business venture.

On returning from his second trip to Russia, Musk set about founding this rocket engine company. He knew he would need someone with expertise in the field if he hoped to make it successful, and in early 2002 he approached Tom Mueller, who at the time worked for TRW Inc. managing the propulsion and combustion products department. TRW is a conglomerate corporation, involved in everything from aerospace technology to credit reporting; Mueller felt the company was so diverse that his ideas were being lost and had started building rocket engines as a hobby.

As a member of the Reaction Research Society (an amateur experimental rocket group based in Southern California) he could launch these engines from their "test site" in the Mojave

Desert. With Musk, though, he could take this interest in rockets to the next level. Mueller left TRW and went to work for Musk as his VP of Propulsion. In June 2002, confident he now had what he needed to succeed, Musk purchased a 75,000 square foot facility in El Segundo, California, and—using a significant chunk of his fortune—and officially founded SpaceX.

Falcon and Dragon development

Of course, building a new, more affordable rocket was not something that could happen overnight. It took seven years for the company to develop its launch vehicles and spacecraft to the point that they could be successfully launched into orbit. Along the way, Musk and his SpaceX employees had to essentially re-invent the way rockets were made to make them lighter and more powerful. Sometimes even the tools to build these things had not yet been created—for the Falcon's airframe, for example, SpaceX engineers designed a machine to friction stir weld aluminum lithium alloy, a machine that didn't yet exist anywhere in the world. New rocket engines were designed along with the launch vehicle, with the Merlin 1D ultimately becoming the engine of choice.

The first launch vehicle designed by SpaceX was called the Falcon 1—one being the number of Merlin 1D engines involved, Falcon being a nod to the Millennium Falcon (Han Solo's famous ship from *Star Wars*). Though they had not figured out how to achieve a vertical landing, all Falcon launch vehicles were designed from the start to be eventually re-usable, something Musk understood would be necessary to the eventual goal of a Mars colony.

Musk obtained permission to use the Ronald Reagan Ballistic Missile Defense Test Site on Omelek Island (part of the Marshall Islands in the South Pacific). From this launch site, the Falcon 1 became the first privately-funded, liquid-propellant rocket to reach orbit in 2008. On July 13, 2009, the company successfully used a Falcon 1 launch vehicle to deliver a satellite into Earth's orbit—another first for a privately-funded rocket company, and the company's first successful commercial payload.

The Falcon 1 launch vehicle was a small rocket; it could carry only a few hundred kilograms into low-Earth orbit, but it was an important first step for the growing company. From 2006 to 2009, Falcon 1 launch vehicles were sent on five separate flights. It succeeded in reaching orbit on its fourth flight; it delivered the satellite on its fifth. However, the Falcon 1 was never where Musk had intended to stop. Now that it had been demonstrated his new rocket engine design would work, SpaceX retired the Falcon 1 and left the distant launch site on Omelek Island, ready to move on to the next stage of their plan.

That next step was the Falcon 9, which had (as the name suggests) nine Merlin 1D engines in its first stage, which can produce a total of 1.3 to 1.5 million pounds of thrust, depending on the launch vehicle's altitude. This made the Falcon 9 an EELV-class medium lift vehicle, capable of carrying over 10,000 kilograms (over 23,000 pounds) into orbit. Working off of the success of the previous Falcon 1 model, the Falcon 9 was able to reach orbit on its first flight attempt in June of 2010.

Between this first launch and the end of 2015, Falcon 9 vehicles were used for 20 successful launches, with only one failure. On December 22, 2015, during the course of a mission to deliver communication satellites for Orbcomm, the first stage of a Falcon 9 launch vehicle was able to return to Cape Canaveral, the world's first successful landing of a rocket used for orbital launch—and one step closer to Musk's ultimate dream of re-usable rockets.

At the same time, they were developing their rocket engines and launch vehicles, SpaceX was also building their spacecraft. Called the Dragon (after Puff the Magic Dragon) this spacecraft is more conventional than their launch vehicle designs. It is a blunt-cone ballistic capsule with a detachable nosecone that's jettisoned shortly after launch for cargo missions. Though that is all it's been used for to date, the Dragon is intended as a crew transport. It has interior space to carry up to seven astronauts into orbit, ultimately with the goal of delivering them to the International Space Station.

The first test of the Dragon's structural integrity took place on June 4, 2010, during the flight of the first Falcon 9 launch vehicle. The first operational Dragon model was launched on December 8 of that year. It made two orbits and then returned to Earth, making SpaceX the first privately-funded company to launch, orbit, and recover a spacecraft. Two years later, on May 25, 2012, a Dragon spacecraft berthed with the International Space Station (the first commercially launched spacecraft to successfully do so). Since this point, the Dragon has made regular resupply runs to and from the ISS.

NASA contracts

Much of the innovation SpaceX accomplished in its first decade was thanks to the contracts they received from NASA. The company's first NASA contract was awarded in 2006, a payment of $278 million intended for SpaceX to develop and test their Falcon 9 launch vehicle, with the ultimate goal of using it to deliver cargo to the International Space Station. Further incentive payments were included in the contract, which would culminate in three demonstration launches set to take place in the latter half of 2008.

As so often happens in the development of new technology, the demonstration launches did not quite go as planned. The first flight, intended to happen in 2008, was delayed several times due to production and supplier issues; it finally occurred on December 8, 2010. A berthing with the ISS wasn't scheduled until the third launch, but after the success of the first the decision was made to do away with the third demonstration launch and berth with the ISS on the second, which took place on May 22, 2012.

SpaceX received its second NASA contract on December 23, 2008. This contract gave the company $1.6 billion in exchange for 12 resupply flights of the Dragon spacecraft (launched using a Falcon 9) to the International Space Station. The idea was to have the Dragon replace the U.S. Space Shuttle after its retirement in 2011. As of April 2016, SpaceX has completed seven of these resupply missions, proving successful in its stated purpose, but the retirement of the Space Shuttle had further-reaching implications that both NASA and SpaceX were well-aware of. Transporting cargo was not the extent of their shared mission; crewed spaceflight was the ultimate goal.

On June 16, 2009, SpaceX announced the opening of its Astronaut Safety and Mission Assurance Department, publically confirming their intention to begin crewed flights of the Dragon spacecraft. Former NASA astronaut Ken Bowersox was hired to oversee the department. Though he would leave the company in 2011, NASA awarded a new contract to SpaceX later that year to develop and demonstrate human-rated Dragon spacecraft as part of their Commercial Crew Development program, showing that the manned mission side of the operation is still very much alive and well. To reinforce this, a second crew transport development contract was offered to SpaceX by NASA in August of 2012.

The immediate intention of this is to allow astronauts to launch from US soil by 2017. Ultimately, the goal from

SpaceX's viewpoint is to make commercial human spaceflight services available to both government and private customers. The 2012 NASA contract gave SpaceX $75 million to develop a human-rated launch escape system, to make and test a crew accommodation mock-up, and to make further progress with the transportation design of the Falcon 9 and Dragon craft. In December 2013, Musk entered negotiations with the Kennedy Space Center in Florida to lease Launch Complex 29A. This new launch complex would be exclusively used for crewed space missions.

In September 2014, NASA chose SpaceX as one of two companies (the other being Boeing) selected to develop systems that would transport U.S. astronauts to and from the International Space Station. This contract, worth $2.6 billion, calls for the Dragon V2 model to be fully human-rated by 2017. Included in the contract is at least one crewed test flight with a NASA astronaut on board. Once the ship is certified, it is intended to conduct between 2 and six crewed missions to the space station.

This is not the only place where NASA's goals align with Elon Musk's. His long-time dream of a human colony on Mars is also on the NASA radar with the conceived mission Red Dragon. Though it had not yet been formally submitted for funding as of September 2015, on April 26, 2016, SpaceX announced its intention to launch a modified Dragon lander to Mars by 2018. The Red Dragon mission will use a Dragon capsule atom a Falcon Heavy launch vehicle to enter the Martian atmosphere. This would not yet be a crewed flight, and certainly not yet a colony; the main objective of this launch will be to bring samples back to Earth. Still, it is Musk's first tangible opportunity to advance his Mars colonization agenda.

The future of SpaceX

The colonization of Mars is the impetus of everything Elon Musk has done in his work thus far with SpaceX; even when his efforts have a seemingly little connection to this ultimate goal, they've later been demonstrated to tie into the project in some tangential—but very important—way. In a 2011 interview, Musk said he hoped to send human beings to the surface of Mars within 10 to 20 years, which would mean between 2021 and 2031. When talking to his biographer, Ashlee Vance, he adjusted this estimate back to 2040, adding that he hopes to establish a colony with a population of around 80,000 people.

Musk sees the exploration of space as a necessary action to preserve and expand the human consciousness. As he pointed out in one interview, natural disasters like volcanoes and asteroids have the potential to wipe out human advancement in an instant, the same way an asteroid is thought to have caused the extinction of the dinosaurs. And, as he points out, we face threats the dinosaurs couldn't even conceive of; genetically engineered viruses, the potentially catastrophic effects of global warming, nuclear disaster, or some new technology we haven't yet conceived ourselves could lead to the decimation of the human population and the collapse of modern society, whether that's through intentional warfare of an unfortunate accident. Musk believes that humans have to expand "beyond this green and blue ball—or go extinct."

While Musk's projects outside the scope of SpaceX (including his work with Tesla Motors developing electric cars and his more recent Hyperloop experiments) are also largely aimed at this ultimate Mars mission, it is through his space-faring company that we can see the biggest push towards his goal. In January of 2005, Musk bought a 10% stake in Surrey Satellite Technology.

Though he had goals for this investment, it was not until nearly a decade later that Musk made his intentions known, when he purchased the SpaceX facility in Seattle, Washington that would construct his conceived global satellite network. In June 2015, Musk asked the federal government for permission to begin testing his satellite project. This network would consist of a constellation of around 4,000 individual satellites and would start its operations in 2020. Though the office staff on the project is starting small, consisting of only 60 engineers, it could expand to over 1,000 workers as the project progresses.

The new launch vehicle currently under design by SpaceX, the Falcon Heavy, is the third and final stage of their launch technology development. As with many aspects of SpaceX's technology development, it has both a short-term commercial purpose and a long-term role in the Mars mission. In the short-term, it will be used to send crewed Dragon spacecraft to the International Space Station. About Mars, the Falcon Heavy will be used to send the colonists on their journey. The Falcon Heavy uses a cluster of three separate Falcon 9 first-stage rockets, giving it a total of 27 Merlin 1D engines; its first demonstration flight is scheduled for November 2016. Alongside the new launch vehicle, SpaceX is also developing a methane-fueled rocket engine, known as the Raptor.

There has been widespread speculation of if (and when) SpaceX would become a publically traded company. A rumor that an IPO was possible by the end of 2013 led Musk to make an announcement in June of that year, stating his plans to hold off on an IPO until the Mars colony is firmly established and the transport flying regularly. He reiterated these plans in 2015, stating it would be many years before SpaceX would be publically traded. Musk's reasoning for this is one of autonomy; he does not want to risk having the company become controlled by "some private equity firm that would milk it for near-term revenue."

Which is not to say that the company does not plan on making money. SpaceX is in no way falling back on its NASA contracts to generate profits. The company plans to open a new commercial-only launch site outside of Brownsville, Texas shortly. They have issued the permit in July of 2014, following the FAA's Environmental Impact Statement for the facility giving it the green light. Construction started in the second half of 2014 and continued through 2015. The first launches are anticipated to take place at the site sometime before the end of 2016.

For centuries, mankind has dreamed of exploring the stars; in this respect, Elon Musk is no different from the rest of us who stare up at the sky and imagine traveling beyond it. Musk had two things, though, that allowed him to turn this common dream into an incredible reality: the financial means acquired through his early forays into internet commerce, and the know-how to accomplished it, based on his lifelong interest in computers and technology. With these two things on his side, Musk established SpaceX as what could quite possibly be the first step in mankind's colonization of space. The idea of human beings walking around—and even living—on another planet within our lifetimes is astounding.

Of course, some delays are likely inevitable, but though SpaceX has encountered delays in nearly every single one of its successful launches so far, it has not yet failed to follow through on its promise to deliver payloads into orbit. Perhaps 2021 is a bit too early to expect interplanetary humanity, but considering how quickly SpaceX developed its Falcon and Dragon technology, 2040 seems more and more reasonable as a colonization date with each new accomplishment SpaceX puts under its belt.

Chapter 6: Tesla Motors

Unlike most of the technological endeavors Elon Musk has undertaken over the course of his life, Tesla Motors was not originally his brainchild. The company was founded in 2003 and operated for a full year before Musk became involved with its operations. Once he joined the team, however, he quickly started making a huge impact on the company's products and operations; by 2009, Musk could be called the *de facto* leader of the automobile company.

Tesla Motors is headquartered in Palo Alto, California. As with SpaceX, it operates both as a production facility for its vehicles and as an Original Equipment Manufacturer for such companies as Daimler, Toyota, and Freightliner. Like with SpaceX, the high degree of vertical integration is very unusual in the automobile industry. In addition to its work on the production end, Tesla Motors maintains its showrooms around the world, selling its products directly to the customer—a very unusual approach in the auto industry, where the standard is for the product to be sold at independent dealerships. It operates a total of 200 stores or galleries around the world, including 120 outside the United States.

Elon Musk has stated that his vision for Tesla Motors is to disrupt the status quo of the automotive industry in a way investor Peter Thiel calls complex coordination—by fitting innovative pieces together in the right way to make products that haven't been possible in the past, at a price that allows them to maintain a high-profit margin. Their primary focus is on pure electric propulsion technology, expanding its capabilities to go further and be viable for a larger segment of the population.

They plan to accomplish this by increasing the number and type of electric vehicles available to mainstream consumers and by selling components of their make to other vehicle manufacturers, inspiring innovation in their products, as well. In that respect, they are very successful; GM vice chairman Robert Lutz said in 2007 that the Tesla Roadster inspired him to develop the Chevrolet Volt, a plug-in hybrid sedan. In keeping with this stated goal, Tesla makes their technology patents available to be used by anyone "in good faith," in the hopes that sharing the technology will encourage other companies to make advancements of their own.

Tesla Motors plays into two of Musk's long-term philosophical goals. The most obvious are its connection to Musk's fight against global warming. By reducing the world's use of combustion engines that rely on fossil fuels, Musk hopes to make a contribution toward the long-term longevity of humankind on the planet Earth, making strides towards reversing the damage traditional automobiles do to the environment—or, at the very least, preventing more irreparable damage from happening.

Not as obvious is the connection of Tesla Motors to his Mars colonization plans. Considering there's no oxygen in the Martian atmosphere, transportation on the planet's surface will need to be electric, not combustion-driven. Like so many of Musk's technological pursuits, the development of electric vehicles can have an immediate goal, purpose, and profitability on Earth—even though it is ultimately intended to serve the Mars colonization effort.

Drawing on his experience in the tech industry, Musk has used a corporate strategy with Tesla Motors very similar to that used in tech product life cycles. This involves a three stage process. First, he planned to enter the market with a high-priced item at low product volume, which Tesla did with the Roadster (which retailed for around $109,000). Step two is a mid-priced vehicle produced at medium product volume, exemplified by both the Model S and the Model X, which sold for about $57,000.

Step three is to enter the low-priced, high-volume market; the Model 3 now in development will be Tesla's entry into that price point, and is expected to sell for around $35,000. The intent here is to aim the early models at affluent "thought leaders" who will spend top dollar for the most innovative products, then use that income as capital to develop less expensive models. This is frequently seen in Silicon Valley with the production of cell phones, laptops, or flat screen televisions. Ultimately, though, Musk plans to have Tesla Motors offer electric cars at prices that make them accessible to the average consumer.

Elon Musk's work on advanced vehicle powertrains has been compared to Henry Ford's work on the Model T for its innovation in the field. Despite being the brains behind the company's most successful products, however, Musk takes very little direct profit from his work with Tesla Motors; as of 2014, his annual salary was only $1. He does receive compensation in the form of performance bonuses and as stock; he owns 28.9 million shares in Tesla, which accounts for about 22% of the company.

Tesla's estimated costs for electric car batteries are some of the lowest in the industry, costing about $200 per kWh. They accomplish this by making their cars differently from other car manufacturers. Rather than using single-purpose, large-format battery cells, Tesla cars use a network of thousands of lithium ion battery cells, the type that is more commonly seen in laptops and cell phones. The cells used by Tesla are specially re-designed to be cheaper and lighter-weight than other consumer batteries, making advancements in this field along with their advancements in the electric auto industry. They have applied this technology to other styles of battery, as well, and work closely with Panasonic to manufacture home and office battery packs and chargers.

In the first quarter of 2013, Tesla posted a profit for the first time in their history. This may seem like a long time to be in the red, but considering their level of innovation is hardly surprising. Their company continues to grow; the company had 3,000 full-time employees in December 2012 and had grown to 13,058 by December 2015. The company sold a total of 125,000 electric cars worldwide between 2008 and March 31, 2016, with the bulk of those sales being of the Model S (119,648 cars).

Founding and early years

As mentioned at the beginning of the chapter, Tesla Motors was not founded by Elon Musk, but by two other entrepreneurs, Martin Eberhard, and Marc Tarpenning. The company gets its name from renowned inventor Nikola Tesla, on whose insights and designs the electric cars of Tesla Motors are based. These two men set up the business in San Carlos, California, developed the early business strategy and financed the project until Musk's arrival.

Elon Musk became the chairman of Tesla's board of directors in February of 2004 and immediately began to take an early role in the company. He led the Series A round of investment that brought in such key investors as Compass Technology Partners and SDL Ventures and became the controlling investor by putting $7.5 million of his personal funds into the company. More importantly, he got very involved in the product development, overseeing the design of the Roadster at a very detailed level.

He was the one who insisted the body be made of carbon fiber reinforced polymer and had a hand in almost every component of the design, from the electronics to the headlamps. Though he was not yet involved in the day to day operations of the business, he had a stronger influence over the company than anyone else involved in this early stage.

It would take more than one round of financing to get Tesla Motors off the ground. The Series B round of financing added Valor Equity Partners as an investor, but was not as successful as the first round, earning only $13 million. The third round of funding that took place in May of 2006, however, brought in an additional $40 million and included investments from major players like Sergey Brin and Larry Page (of Google fame), Jeff Skoll (former president of eBay), and Nick Prizker (the heir to the Hyatt fortune). Several venture capital firms also took an interest in this round, with investments coming in from Capricorn Management, Draper Fisher Jurveston, and the Bay Area Equity Fund.

The increase in interest was no doubt related to the fact that Tesla Motors finally had a product to show potential investors; the first prototype of the Tesla Roadster was introduced to the public that year. It went on sale in the fall of 2007 following a fourth round of financing that added $45 million more to the company. All told, Elon Musk raised $105 million in private financing for Tesla Motors in his first three years of involvement with the company.

Leadership through crisis

Though they'd developed their first product, Tesla Motors was not a complete financial success, even with the magnitude of funding Musk had secured. The company opened an office in Rochester Hills, Michigan in 2007, an investment of funds that would ultimately prove unsuccessful; that office would close shortly after that. There was also significant upheaval within the company at this time. Original CEO Martin Eberhard was asked to resign by the board of directors in August of 2007, briefly instead taking the title of President of Technology before leaving the company entirely in January of 2008, a rather messy affair that would result in later lawsuits against Musk about the manner in which Eberhard left the company. Ze'ev Drori was hired to replace Eberhard in December of 2007.

This would prove only to be the beginning of the two roughest years in Tesla Motors' history to that point. In his new role as CEO, Drori gave the entire staff performance reviews, ultimately firing key personnel in January of 2008, many of whom had been involved with the company since its beginning. All told, the company's workforce was reduced by about 10%. The remaining co-founder, Marc Tarpenning, left the company shortly after that.

The business collapses that would lead to the worldwide economic recession of 2007-2008 were hard on many companies, small and large—and Tesla Motors was exactly the kind of company that should have been hit hard, perhaps even driven to bankruptcy, by the crisis. After all, they were still in stage one of their three-step process, marketing their Roadster (the ultimate luxury item) to the same people who had lost the most in the course of the crash. Despite this, Tesla continued to push forward with their business plans, opening their first retail store in Los Angeles in April of 2008, with a second to follow in Menlo Park, California in July.

In October, Musk took over as CEO of the company, though Ze'ev Drori had held the position for less than a year; Drori would step down to vice chairman until December 2008, when he left the company for good.

Similar to Drori's take over as CEO the previous year, Musk's first act was to fire significant chunks of Tesla Motor's staff—this time around a quarter of the full-time employees.

Unlike Drori, Musk also took over as product architect and undertook the fifth round of financing, adding another $40 million to the overall investments. This pulled Tesla Motors back from the brink of bankruptcy, but certainly did not yet have them on stable footing. By January of 2009, Tesla had raised $187 million (including $70 million of Musk's money) and delivered only 147 cars; Musk's idea of an affordable and viable electric car seemed just as far away as ever.

The summer of 2009 saw this rough patch in Tesla Motors' history finally coming to an end. They unveiled plans for their new Model S on March 26, 2009, then secured $465 million in interest-bearing loans from the U.S. Department of Energy to support the engineering and production of the new model, along with new commercial powertrain technology. These loans were not the same as the bailout funds given to major auto manufacturers like GM and Chrysler; Tesla did repay the loan in May of 2013, the first car company to fully repay the loan given to them by the federal government.

In May of 2009, Daimler acquired an equity stake in Tesla Motors, securing around 10% of the company for $50 million. All of these extra finances certainly helped; in August of 2009, Tesla Motors announced that it had achieved overall profitability for the previous month.

Though things were certainly looking up for the company, the dark cloud of their lean years had not quite completely passed. Former CEO Martin Eberhard sued both Tesla Motors and Elan Musk for breach of contract, slander, and libel. The suit was filed on May 26, 2009. Musk's response to this was to take to social media, documenting in a blog post why Eberhard had been fired and posting proof that the decision had been undertaken unanimously by the entire board of directors. After a San Mateo County judge had stricken down Eberhard's claim to be declared one of only two company founders for Tesla Motors, he withdrew his suit in early August of 2009, reaching a final settlement with Musk on September 21. With the old drama now completely under the bridge, Musk moved forward with his plans to push the company to the next level.

Going public

On June 29, 2010, Tesla Motors launched its Initial Public Offering on the NASDAQ stock exchange. Just over 13 million shares were issued to the public at a cost of $17 per share. This made Tesla Motors the first American automobile manufacturer to go public since Ford had its IPO back in 1956; Tesla's IPO raised a total of $226 million in capital for the company.

Shortly after this, in July of 2010, former Apple executive George Blankenship was hired as Vice President of Design and Store Development. The purpose of bringing him on was to build Tesla's retail strategy further. He would leave the company in 2013, but not before designing a series of retail outlets for worldwide distribution of Tesla's cars directly to their customers.

This new design of retail stores would feature interactive displays and design studios to customize Model S's before purchase; customers could view their creations on an 85-inch display wall. These stores would open worldwide over the next few years. In June 2009, their first European store opened in London's Knightsbridge district; their first continental European store opened in Munich in September 2009. Their first store in Asia opened in Aoyama, Japan in November 2010; a Sydney showroom in Australia also opened that year.

Along with the opening of their new stores, Tesla Motors moved its corporate headquarters in 2010 to the Stanford Research Park in Palo Alto, a project partially financed by the loans they'd previously received from the federal government.

This new facility was a 369,000 square foot structure on a 23-acre plot of land, a much larger structure suggesting the business was gearing up for further growth. Though the initial plan called for 350 employees, there was room left for this to grow up to 650 in the next few years. The lean years of Tesla Motors were over; from this point out, growth would be the rule of the land.

The Tesla Roadster

The Roadster's motor is a direct descendant of Nikola Tesla's 1882 design—though significantly updated for the modern world. In the years since its initial release, it has broken the mold on the electric car and had some firsts to its name. It was the first car manufactured by Tesla Motors and the first electric sports car ever developed. It was also the first production automobile that used lithium ion battery cells, the first production electric vehicle with a range of more than 200 miles per charge, and the first highway-capable all-electric vehicle to go into serial production. Around 2,500 Roadsters were sold between its introduction and the end of its product run in 2012, which were sold in 31 countries.

The first prototypes of the Roadster were introduced to the public in July of 2006. Though it was not available for public use until the following year, the Roadster was featured on the cover of *Time Magazine* in December of 2006 as the best transportation invention of the year. A limited production run of 100 vehicles was released in 2007; it sold out within three weeks, with the second run of 100 selling out by October of that year. General production started on March 17, 2008, with later models introduced in 2009 and 2010.

The Roadster used a carbon fiber body to lessen its weight and increase its top speed. It is an impressive sports car by any standards, competing with traditional automobiles in a way that electric vehicles had never been able to before. It can go from 0-

60 in 3.7 seconds and has a top speed of 125 miles per hour. Among electric vehicles, its long charge life stands out, with an average range of 245 miles per charge and the potential for more. On October 27, 2009, a Roadster was driven by Simon Hackett drove 313 miles of Australia's Global Green Challenge on a single charge, going an average speed of 25 miles per hour. Based on these statistics, *Motor Times* called Tesla "the first maker to crack the EV legitimacy barrier in a century."

The production of the Roadster was cut unexpectedly short as a result of a supply issue that arose in 2011. Tesla Motors had been in a production contract with Group Lotus for the gliders of the Roadsters since 2005. This contract initially only ran through March of 2011; though it was extended through December of 2011, changes in the tooling of Group Lotus made the Roadster gliders permanently unavailable.

The final limited production run of the original Roadster was completed in early 2012, to be distributed only in Europe, Asia, and Australia. A next generation Roadster is in the works, though it is a lower priority than the lower-cost models currently in production; the next generation Roadster is expected to be introduced in 2019.

Model S

The second stage of Tesla Motors' overarching plan started with the production and release of the Model S, Tesla's entry into the four-door sedan model. The Model S was announced on June 30, 2008, and unveiled to the public on March 26, 2009; customer deliveries started in June of 2012. Some changes were made to the overall design of the Model S as compared to the Roadster, some of which were aimed at addressing issues with the previous model, others of which were a natural byproduct of the shift in purpose. The battery pack in the Roadster was behind the seats; in the Model S, it was integrated into the floor, increasing the vehicle's interior and trunk space. The new location also made it easier to swap out the battery, a process that in the Model S can take as little as 90 seconds. Also unlike the Roadster, the Model S used an aluminum body, slightly reducing its top speed but increasing safety and durability.

The Model S was available in two models: one with an 85 kWh battery with an average range of 265 miles per charge, and another with a 60 kWh battery that gets an average of 208 miles per charge. These cars were among the first manufactured at the new Tesla Factory that opened in October of 2010 in Fremont, California. Delivery of Model S sedans began on June 22, 2012, in the United States. It became available in Europe a little over a year later, in August of 2013, and reached the Asian market in April of 2014.

On October 1, 2013, just over a year after its initial release, a Model S driving on a highway in Kent, Washington had its battery pack catch fire after hitting metal debris along the roadway. The fire was isolated to a small section of the vehicle's battery pack and the driver left the car uninjured, but the incident alarmed customers and shareholders alike. The price on Tesla Motors shares dropped about 12% in the two days following the accident, though it recovered slightly in the ensuing week. The second incident occurred shortly after that; when the third battery fire happened, Tesla realized it had a problem on its hands. Their stock, which had only started to recover from the first fire, dropped an additional 20%.

In each of the cases where a fire had occurred in the battery packs of Tesla Model S's, significant road debris was struck at highway speeds and ricocheted into the under-car battery pack. The new placement of the battery was responsible for the vulnerability, and the reason these issues had not cropped up before on Roadster models. Rather than rearrange the design to move the battery pack deeper into the car's engine (or back behind the seats, as it had been in the Roadster) Tesla created a new battery protection system, putting an aluminum alloy armor plate around the underside of the battery pack to protect it from impacts. This protection system was installed on all new Model S's produced and issued as a no-cost retrofit to all that had already been purchased.

Aside from this fire-related hiccup—and indeed, even through it—the Model S performed extremely well in both domestic and foreign markets, far exceeding the sales and popularity of the Roadster. Even in 2013 when the issues with the battery were taking place, Tesla Motors was a top performer on the NASDAQ 100 index. Sales of the Model S in 2013 totaled over 22,000 in Europe and North America.

It was also the first electric car to top the monthly sales ranking in any country, reaching first place for car sales in Norway for September 2013 (not incidentally, Norway is the Model S's largest overseas market, with over 10,000 units sold there as of December 2015). The potential safety issue with the battery also didn't stop the Model S from raking in its fair share of awards. In 2013, it won both the Motor Trend Car of the Year and the World Green Car awards; Elon Musk also received several personal awards for his design of the vehicle.

Since it was not plagued by supplier issues as the Roadster was, the Model S has enjoyed a sustained production run since its introduction. The 2015 sales year is especially good for it; sales within the United States passed the 50,000 unit milestone for total sales in July of 2015, while global sales surpassed 100,000 in December of that same year.

Global sales of the Model S in 2015 were over 50,000, making it the best-selling plug-in electric vehicle for the year. As of December 2015, it ranked second on the all-time list for best-selling plug-in cars behind the Nissan Leaf. By June of 2015, drivers of the Model S had accumulated over 1 billion electric miles, making the Model S the first plug-in electric vehicle fleet of any make or type to pass that impressive milestone.

Model X

The other half of Tesla Motor's second phase of production was the Model X, its entry into the SUV/minivan market. It was unveiled on February 9, 2012, although the launch was delayed and deliveries did not begin until September of 2015. Like the Model S, this full-size crossover SUV uses an aluminum body and an under-floor battery pack.

Deliveries in the first full year of the Model X's production were delayed because of supplier parts shortages, but the sales figures were still impressive. Almost 3,000 vehicles were sold between September 2015 and April 2016—a lower figure than for the Model S, to be sure, but impressive considering the production delays the model has experienced.

Model 3

With both the Model S and the Model X doing well in the global market, Tesla Motors turned its attention to the third stage of its production process—the low-price and high-volume entry into the general consumer market that would start with the Model 3. First unveiled on March 31, 2016, the delivery of vehicles is expected to begin by the end of 2017, with a price set to start at $35,000 before any applicable government incentives.

The public response to the announcement of the Model 3 has been impressive. The company announced that it would be possible to make reservations on Model 3s at Tesla stores worldwide with a refundable $1,000 deposit. Within one week of the product's unveiling, the company had received 325,000 reservations—more units than the Model S had sold for its entire production life up to that point. The largest proportion of the reservations came from the United States, though a significant number of the reservations also came in from China, a relatively recent addition to Tesla's market. Extrapolating from the expected price, these reservations could potentially equate to $14 billion in global sales.

Few details about the Model 3 have been released to the public. The details of the design and composition of the body are still unknown. Conventional auto manufacturer wisdom says that steel is the most cost-effective material. Tesla Motors has recently purchased a new aluminum stamping press for its factory, however, leading many to believe they'll continue to use an aluminum body for their Model 3 as they had for the Model S and Model X. Although 2017 is the stated date for retail sales, the incredible demand in reservations means they probably won't be able to fulfill the expected demand and have available units for open sale until as late as 2020.

Charging stations

As traditional combustion engine automobiles need a well-established network of gas stations to undertake lengthy journeys, so to do electric cars need a network of charging stations if their drivers want to go further than their home city. In 2012, Tesla Motors began work on a network of 480-volt Supercharger stations. These stations are designed to charge plug-in cars more quickly than traditional chargers, letting them get back on the road more quickly to enable long road trips without the need for overnight stays.

A Supercharger station can give a Model S an additional 170 miles of charge in about 30 minutes, or a full charge in 75. The electricity for the Superchargers in warmer climates is provided by a solar carport system built by SolarCity (another of

Musk's side-projects); the eventual goal is for these Supercharger stations to be all-solar world-wide.

The first Supercharger corridor was established in October 2012. It featured six stations along the corridor between Los Angeles, Los Vegas, San Francisco, and Lake Tahoe. Two months later, in December 2012, a second American corridor was opened in the northeast, with three stations connecting Baltimore, Philadelphia, New York City, Boston, and Washington, DC. After these initial experiments proved successful, Tesla dramatically accelerated its Supercharger network development. It added Superchargers to Europe and Asian markets in late 2013 and increased the number of stations available in North America, though the emphasis remained on the costs. As of May 20, 2016, a total of 624 stations had been built worldwide, with 259 in North America, 222 in Europe, and the remainder in the Asia and Pacific region.

As a part of this expansion of their charger network, Tesla Motors introduced their Destination Charging Location network in 2014. This system uses chargers that aren't quite as powerful as the Supercharger network but still give twice the charging power of a traditional station, strategically located in places where Musk says his customers "spend the most time," including upscale shops, restaurants, hotels, and resorts. Following the success of this system in North America, a European destination charging network was established in April of 2016. Tesla also started partnering with Airbnb in August of 2015, providing chargers at host houses in California with plans to expand across the nation and the world.

Tesla Motors into the future

In the third quarter of 2015, Tesla Motors produced 13,901 vehicles—the most for any quarter to date. Based on the demand indicated by the initial reservation numbers on the Model 3,

Tesla announced an advanced build plan in May of 2016 that would have them putting out 500,000 total units in 2018, two years earlier than that level of demand had been planned. In response to this increased demand across the globe, Tesla has started negotiations to open factories in Europe, India, and China to help meet the demand in those markets. Musk has said that the bulk of production will remain in the United States for the foreseeable future; the factories that open on other continents will be based solely on demand.

Elon Musk is never one to sit still and bask in his accomplishments. As well as the current models released from Tesla Motors are doing, there are already plans for new designs in the company's Hopper. The possibility of a truck has been under consideration since 2012, though no specific plans for development have been announced. Fleet vans for use by municipal governments are another vehicle style under discussion. At least one future model has been officially announced—the Model Y, described to the public in October 2015. This will combine the crossover SUV design of the Model X with the price point of the Model 3.

Little is known of the design aside from the fact that it will feature falcon wing doors. Future models are also expected to expand on and advance the industry's autonomous driving functions. Musk believes cars will have the ability to drive themselves within a six-year time frame, though he is quick to add that it will take several more years for industry guidelines to be laid down that would allow a broad embrace of this innovation.

The first four models developed by Tesla Motors utilized battery cells made by Panasonic. In August of 2014, Musk announced plans to establish a Giga factory near Reno, Nevada to begin constructing their batteries. This factory will be run in conjunction with Panasonic; they are not abandoning that connection completely, but rather shifting their efforts to include the production of batteries as part of their vertical integration system. This new factory will employ 6,500 people and is slated to open for production in late 2016 or early 2017.

By making their battery systems in-house, Tesla expects to cut costs of batteries by 30%; it is unclear what effect this will have on the pricing of their various plug-in cars. Beyond the price considerations, the expansion of their business to include the production of batteries will also allow innovations. A patented battery system is already under development to pair metal-air and lithium ion batteries, potentially increasing the miles per charge to 500 or more in future car models. In addition to their work on car batteries, the Reno factory will produce their new Powerwall line of home and industrial batteries, which will be made utilizing a similar technology.

Elon Musk is an expert businessman as well as a technological innovator. It is reasonable to expect innovations in that aspect of the company, as well, as it moves forward. One example of this is the start of their "certified pre-owned" buyback program. Launched in May of 2015, this program allows those who buy the Tesla Model S to return it to Tesla after three years of ownership in exchange for a reimbursement of 43-50% of the original price. The aim is to secure a steady supply of used cars that can be refurbished and sold second-hand from official Tesla stores.

As with many things Elan Musk does in his businesses, the goal here is two sided. On the one hand, it serves to fulfill that aim of providing affordable plug-in cars for the mass market consumer; the pricing on the used Model S's is much more amenable to a working class income. On the other hand, it is been shown through buyback programs of traditional auto manufacturers that the profit margin on a used car is about three times that on a new car. Introducing a buyback program allows Tesla to sell the same car two or even three times over the course of its life, a prospect with enormous profit potential.

As of July 2015, there were only about 250 used Model S's in the company's buyback program, but this number is expected to increase. Similar programs have also been introduced in Canada, and in several European nations.

Chapter 7: Technological Innovations

Between them, Tesla Motors and SpaceX would be enough business and innovation for even your typical ambitious entrepreneur. As Elon Musk has made clear at several points throughout his life, however, he is in no way a typical entrepreneur. Musk's work outside of his two main businesses has a similar set of goals and ideologies: to nudge humanity towards a more sustainable way of life and to continue developing the technologies that will be needed to sustain new human colonies on other planets. In many cases, Musk's side projects serve both of these goals, in one way or another.

Collaborations between Musk's side projects and his two main businesses are also so common as to be called the norm. The use of SolarCity panels to power Tesla Motors Supercharger stations is just one example of this cross-company infrastructure. SpaceX and Tesla are both heavily involved in the development of the Hyperloop, one of Musk's more recent and intriguing projects. Indeed, the entirety of Musk's career post-PayPal can be seen as an ever-expanding network of vertical and horizontal integrations—one that ultimately tells the story of one man's quest to fulfill an impossible and life-long dream.

SolarCity

SolarCity was co-founded in 2006 by brothers Lyndon and Peter Rive—who just happen to be Musk's maternal cousins. Though Elon Musk is not officially involved with the company's operations, he did provide both the original concept and the financial backing to get SolarCity off the ground and remains to this day the company's largest shareholder.

The underlying motivation behind SolarCity is to help combat global warming by providing reliable and sustainable energy for both residential and industrial use. Headquartered in San Mateo, California, SolarCity is the second-largest solar system provider in the United States, with over 13,000 employees and plans to expand even more in the coming years. It has been the leading provider of residential solar power in California since its first full year of operation in 2007. On the industrial side, SolarCity has built projects for such corporations as Walmart, Intel, and the U.S. military. It is also one of the founding members of The Alliance for Solar Choice (TASC), the nation's leading solar advocacy organization.

Regarding SolarCity's interaction with other companies under Elon Musk's umbrella, the provision of solar power to Tesla Motors' Supercharger stations is just the tip of the iceberg. A program started in 2013 has SolarCity collaborating with Tesla to use their electric car batteries to smooth the impact of rooftop solar installations on the power grid. The Powerwall battery devices being made at the new Tesla Giga factory in Nevada will be utilized by SolarCity as backup storage with future photovoltaic installations.

They've also announced that a network of electric car chargers will be installed in all of their service areas, and have teamed up with Rabobank to make electric car charging stations available free to Tesla owners driving along Route 101 in California; SolarCity entered the electric car charging industry all the way back in 2009, when it purchased SolSource Energy (once part of Clean Fuel Connections, Inc.).

Diversification has been the theme of SolarCity's business model nearly since the start of its operation. They entered the solar leasing market in 2008, allowing homeowners to switch to solar power relatively risk-free while still paying less for energy each month than they would go only through the utility company. In 2010, they acquired Building Solutions, a business dedicated to home energy audits, and used this company's infrastructure to offer energy efficiency evaluations and upgrades to its customers.

In 2013, they purchased Zep Solar, a company known for their mounting technologies. The system they'd developed was constructed of "snap together" panels that eliminated the need for mountain rails on most rooftops. This quick and easy installation help to make SolarCity's panels available in a more convenient package to a wider range of customers.

Along with buying up other companies, SolarCity has achieved some significant building projects and accolades all its own. In May of 2008, the company completed an installation of solar panels on eBay's North Campus in San Jose—at the time the largest commercial solar installation in the United States. Two months later, SolarCity broke their record with an even larger installation (consisting of over 1,600 photovoltaic panels) at British Motor Car Distributors in San Francisco. The SolarStrong project, announced late in 2011, is the company's largest undertaking to date.

This five-year project would build over $1 billion in photovoltaic panels for military housing communities. With an ultimate output of 300 megawatts—enough to power up to 120,000 individual housing units—SolarStrong will be the largest residential solar project in national history upon its completion. To help them meet ever-increasing demand, SolarCity announced plans in June of 2014 to build a new manufacturing facility in Buffalo, New York. The factory is expected to produce around one gigawatt of solar panels each year and will be three times the size of the nation's current largest solar plant. The factory was set to open in early 2016;

due to difficulties ordering machinery, that opening date was pushed back to the summer of 2017.

Though he has no official role in the operational side of SolarCity, Elon Musk is the chairman of the company's charitable arm, the Musk Foundation, which directs its philanthropic efforts on providing solar power systems to disaster areas. After Japan had been hit by devastating tsunamis in 2011, the Musk Foundation donated over $250,000 to go to the construction of a solar network in Soma, one of the areas ravaged by the storms. The foundation has also done impressive work domestically, donating solar power systems to hurricane response centers, such as the South Bay Community Alliance's Center in Coden, Alabama.

Hyperloop

The Hyperloop program was designed by a collaboration of engineers from both Tesla Motors and SpaceX—which makes sense, as it combines aspects of both companies. On the one hand, it is a transportation system that could revolutionize the way humans travel around the world; on the other; it is one of Musk's projects that's more obviously aimed at the future Mars colony. Given that the atmosphere of Mars has a density that's about 1% that of the Earth's, air resistance and friction will not be impediments to travel there. The technology being developed for the Hyperloop could be directly translated to the red planet without the need for vacuum tubes, meaning it is technology in many ways better suited to Mars than to our home planet.

The Hyperloop is a theoretical high-speed transportation system that uses a combination of linear inductor motors and air compressors to float pressurized capsules down rails, in a similar way to how a puck is moved across an air hockey table. This avoids the use of magnetic levitation while still allowing speeds greater than what wheels can handle. Linear induction motors would be utilized along the tube to accelerate or slow down the capsules, which would otherwise be able to glide for the majority of the journey, eliminating any rolling resistance.

The big development in the Hyperloop is the partial vacuum tubes the rails and pods will run through. In the past, the main impediment to high-speed rail systems was the air resistance factor. By introducing a partial vacuum to the tubes surrounding the track, the Hyperloop will avoid friction and air resistance, allowing travel at higher speeds with lower energy usage—if a vacuum can in fact be maintained over such a long distance. The idea of using evacuated tubes for train travel was first introduced over a century ago, but the technology has never been in place that would allow such a system to work. With two groundbreaking corporations—and their innumerable engineers—at his back, Musk believes he can overcome this challenge that has prevented similar concepts from coming to life in the past.

The first designs were published on the Tesla and SpaceX blogs in 2013, with initial design testing just taking place at the time of this writing in May of 2016. Like many of Musk's technological developments, Hyperloop is explicitly open-source, and he actively encourages other inventors to take the ideas and develop them further. With Hyperloop, Musk has even gone one step further, opening up a design competition for student engineers to make their Hyperloop pods and test them at a track operated and sponsored by SpaceX.

The competition was first announced in June of 2015; within a month, more than 700 teams had submitted preliminary applications, before the official and detailed rules were even distributed in August. At a design briefing in November of 2015, the field was pared down to 120 engineering teams, who were invited to submit their final design packages at a weekend conference held at Texas A&M at the end of January 2016. A group of engineers from MIT were named the winners of the design side of the contest, followed by a team from Delft University in the Netherlands. All told, 22 teams were invited to build and test their pods at the competition, which will be held in August of 2016.

The student competitions will not be the first tests of the technology to take place. That honor goes to Hyperloop One, a company founded by venture capitalist Shervin Pishevar and SpaceX lead engineer Brogan BamBrogan. Their plan is to develop a route between Los Angeles and Las Vegas, and they have raised over $35 million in working capital towards this goal. With a board of directors and a team of over 100 engineers already in place, Hyperloop One is currently building the most advanced and viable Hyperloop technology in the world. In May of 2016, they conducted their first test of the electric motor technology, which powered a test sled for this first demonstration. The test vehicle ran for only a few seconds on a 1/3 mile track outside of Las Vegas, but this test is the first step in what is arguably the most important transportation technology development since the design of the combustion engine.

In addition to Hyperloop One, two other major organizations have undertaken the development of Musk's technology. Hyperloop Transportation Technologies is a group of around 500 engineers from across the United States, who collaborate through weekly teleconferences. The members work for stock options only and believe they are still about a decade away from opening a commercially operating Hyperloop, but they are exploring route options. The group purchased a 5-mile plot of land in California, alongside a road that connects Los Angeles to San Francisco, with the intent of building a test track for Hyperloop pods.

Construction on the project began in November of 2015 in conjunction with Oerlikon Leybold Vacuum and AECOM. The Canadian company TransPod is focused more on the vehicles than on the track. They announced a new pod design in March 2016 and will be developing a full-scale concept vehicle to show at the InnoTrans Rail Show in Berlin in September of 2016. Their hope is to produce commercially viable pods by the year 2020, with the eventual goal of establishing a Hyperloop line between Montreal and Toronto.

The idea of the Hyperloop is to not only build a faster way to get from place to place, but also to design a method of transportation that's immune to weather conditions, is not in danger of experiencing collisions, and has relatively low power requirements to reduce the carbon foothold. Musk anticipates later versions of the technology reaching or exceeding sonic speeds, though the low air pressure within the tubes should prevent the accompanying sonic boom. Musk believes the tunnel system could be constructed either above or below ground, with the pods expected to be around 7.5 feet in diameter.

In addition to the Los Angeles to Las Vegas route proposed by Hyperloop One, there are several other national routes being considered. The original design put forth by SpaceX called for a route connecting Los Angeles to San Francisco. Their estimated budget for this project is around $6 billion; the route would parallel Interstate 5, with an anticipated travel time of 35 minutes at an average speed of 600 miles per hour. Branches built off of this main route would also connect cities like Sacramento, Anaheim, San Diego, and Las Vegas into the network. European developers are also getting in on the action. In January 2016, Dutch company Delft Hyperloop proposed a route that would connect Paris to Amsterdam. A team from the Warsaw University of Technology is also evaluating the feasibility of a route across Poland, connecting Cracow to Gdansk.

The Hyperloop project has drawn much attention, much of it is skeptical. The Ansys Corporation ran several fluid dynamics simulations meant to model the stress forces and aerodynamics of Hyperloop capsules. According to their findings, the suggested tube diameter is too narrow; the currently proposed designs would need to be tweaked to avoid supersonic airflow. Though they found some issues with the details of the design, however, their overall assessment of the project labeled it as feasible. A development team with OpenMDAO released a conceptual model of the Hyperloop's propulsion system in October 2013.

As with Ansys' findings, OpenMDAO's analysis said the project was feasible but in need of some adjustment. Their model called for a 13-foot diameter tube, a much larger design than in the original projections. A second study done by the same company reiterated the need for a larger tube and made more specific recommendations about the design, including the removal of on-board heat exchangers to reduce weight in the pod.

Much of the criticism of the Hyperloop project is centered around the rider experience. The pods are, by design, windowless and narrow. Both the pod and the track will need to be thoroughly sealed, potentially generating an uncomfortable level of noise. The acceleration may also be a factor. Even the most optimistic estimates put the inertial acceleration factor at two to three times that of the takeoff or landing of a commercial airliner. MathWorks did an analysis of the Hyperloop technology in November 2013 focused primarily on the passenger experience. Though they found the project to be feasible, they did express concerns about the effects of the acceleration.

The early cost estimates put out by SpaceX have also come into question. The alpha project designs suggested an end-user cost of $20 per one-way ticket from Los Angeles to San Francisco, but many believe this is far too low to make the Hyperloop a viable and self-sustaining option. The initial construction budget of $6 billion has also been criticized as far too optimistic an estimate. Considering the amount of work that still needs to be done on the development and testing—not to mention the scope of the construction that will be required for just one of the national routes—many economic experts have asserted that this estimated budget is a gross under-estimate.

Because Elon Musk is settled in California, most of the early route suggestions have been in the state, or at least the Southwest United States region. As convenient as this is the concept's founder, the truth is that California may not be the most amenable option when it comes time seriously to consider the construction of a Hyperloop system. The long-running High-Speed Rail project already underway in California has already seen a lot of time, money, and "reputational capital," as it were, invested into it. Replacing that with the Hyperloop project—which will remain untested as a commercial venture for some time yet—is not likely to go over well in some political circles.

SpaceX already has strong ties to Texas, and that has been suggested as an alternate location for the first operational Hyperloop system. The political environment there may prove friendlier to the introduction of the Hyperloop; the landscape may also prove more viable for initial construction.

It is worth noting that, while there have been some questions about the economic feasibility and the exact dimensions of the system that will be put into place, no one has yet pointed out any reason why this form of transportation would be impossible. Much of the squabbling concerns the vacuum tubes that will reduce the air friction enough to make such high speeds possible. Regardless of if and when the first commercial Hyperloop opens, it is most certainly already a viable option for an environment that lacks an atmosphere. Even if the Hyperloop never becomes a reality here on planet Earth, the availability of a tested and proven high-speed transportation technology that will work on the surface of Mars will no doubt serve as suitable consolation for the concept's founder.

Open AI

One of Elon Musk's most recent side projects is a bit of a departure for him. It still has to do with what some would call "science fiction" technology—the much-beloved and much-debated concept of artificial intelligence—but is rare in that it has no obvious connection to his eventual colonization of Mars.

OpenAI was created in December of 2015. It is a not for profit research company aimed at the development of artificial intelligence in a manner that's both safe and beneficial for humanity. Musk's stated goals for the company are to work against big corporations that could use super-intelligent computer systems exclusively for profit, as well as to prevent government organizations from using AI to "gain power and even oppress their citizenry." In the past, Musk has frequently spoken out about the potential dangers of artificial intelligence. He has alternatively called artificial intelligence "summoning the demon" and "the most serious threat to the survival of the human race." In an interview at MIT's AeroAstro Centennial Symposium, Musk said he's increasingly convinced there should be regulatory oversight regarding AI, "just to make sure that we do not do something very foolish."

Despite his apparent opposition to the development of AI, Musk has become increasingly involved with its creation. He invested in both the AI firm DeepMind and Vicarious, a company that works to improve machine intelligence. In January of 2015, he donated $10 million to the Future of Life Institute, an organization whose focus is on overcoming the challenges posed by advanced technology. Musk has stated that these investments in artificial intelligence are less about trying to make it a reality, and not even necessarily about generating a return on his investment, but more as a way for him to monitor what's happening in the world of artificial intelligence and attempt to nudge it in a direction that will make it beneficial—rather than harmful—to humanity.

Like most of Musk's endeavors, OpenAI is open source and aims to collaborate freely with other research institutions by making all of its patents open to the public. Unlike Musk's other business ventures, OpenAI is a non-profit. This decision was motivated by Musk's inherent distrust of the concept of artificial intelligence—he wanted to keep it free from any stockholder obligations to make sure the focus stays on AI research that will have long-term positive incomes on humanity, rather than becoming motivated by profit. The employees and board members of the company by and large share Musk's unease with the concept of artificial intelligence and are primarily motivated by these concerns.

They also agree that research on AI cannot be avoided; the best tactic to keep it from being misused, in the minds of Musk and others, is to make sure it stays available to the broadest cross-section of society possible so that no individual or company can gain "AI superpower." This approach is somewhat controversial among those who share Musk's concerns about the potential harm of human-level artificial intelligence. Philosopher Nick Bostrom summed up the skepticism in an April 2016 interview with *Wired*, saying "If you have a button that could do bad things to the world, you do not want to give it to everyone."

OpenAI is less than six months old at the time of writing, meaning it is difficult to evaluate what impact it will have on the development and distribution of artificial intelligence at this point. Their only action so far has been the public release of the beta version of their OpenAI gym. This platform aims to standardize the way environments are defined in AI publications so that the research can be more easily reproduced by others. Future projects can be expected to stay in this same vein, generally staying more concerned with expanding the access to artificial intelligence research than doing large quantities of development in the field themselves.

Chapter 8 – His Greatest Inspirations

When people ask Elon how he was able to learn how to build rockets, his answer is always simple.

"I read a lot of books."

Books have remained important to Elon and his love for reading came about because of his childhood. He was often bullied (he was lumbered with the school nickname, Muskrat because of his appearance) and buried himself in literature, especially sci-fi in order to escape the pain of his everyday life. There are many writers who inspired Elon but the two that shaped his life were J.R.R Tolkien and Isaac Asimov and he often submerged himself in their work as a means to cope. However, his love for books has always been central in his life and as we're about to see, he often looked for stories with great heroes on which he could model himself. In turn, this gave him the inspiration to embark on his scientific endeavors.

1. THE LORD OF THE RINGS by J.R.R. Tolkien

One of the first books to inspire him and shape his identity, Lord of the Rings showed him that good could overcome evil and that people could triumph over the impossible. It taught him that people could achieve the extraordinary and he had often said that heroes in fantasy books such as Frodo in the Lord of the Rings had a tremendous sense of duty to save the world, something that he could identify with.

2. 'Benjamin Franklin: An American Life' by Walter Isaacson

Aside from Frodo, Elon thought of Benjamin Franklin as another one of his great heroes, stating that he was one of the earliest and greatest entrepreneurs.

"He was an entrepreneur. He started from nothing. He was just a runaway kid," he says. "He was pretty awesome."

It would seem that Franklin's rags to riches tale inspired Elon to follow in his footsteps, rising through the scientific ranks through his move from Pretoria, to Canada through to Silicon Valley.

3. 'Structures: Or Why Things Don't Fall Down' by J.E. Gordon

If there ever is a way to learn rocket science from a book, reading Structures is maybe the closest way. So when Elon embarked on a journey to create SpaceX, his first point of reference was this book which he describes as "Really, really good if you want a primer on structural design."

Unlike the above, this scientific book by British material scientist, J.E. Gordon may not have a hero in which to draw inspiration from but it certainly equipped Elon with the practical tools he needed to begin his quest with SpaceX.

4. 'The Hitchhiker's Guide to the Galaxy' by Douglas Adams

Like many people who have an existential crisis in their younger years, Elon had his own when he was fifteen. In an attempt to discover the meaning of life, he delved into the philosophical works of Nietzsche and Schopenhauer but only found himself more confused.

Luckily, he stumbled across Douglas Adams' classic in which the meaning of life is discovered to be the number 42, although the question is never known. This may not have been useful to most people but young Elon thought this to be incredibly helpful saying:

"If you can properly phrase the question, then the answer is the easy part. So, to the degree that we can better understand the universe, then we can better know what questions to ask."

5. 'Einstein: His Life and Universe' by Walter Isaacson

Einstein might seem like an obvious source of inspiration for a great scientific mind like Elon, especially as they are both seen to have highly progressive, original ideas with a flair for envisioning the seemingly impossible. They were also both dedicated to transforming the world with their desire to advance humanity through scientific discovery.

6. 'Ignition!: An Informal History of Liquid Rocket Propellants' by John D. Clark

This rarely accessible account of early rocket science dates back to the 1960s and depicts not only the scientific techniques and theories needed to understand rocket propulsion but also discusses the politics involved with such a complicated and delicate science. Despite its complexity, Elon describes it as "really fun".

7. 'Zero to One: Notes on Startups, or How to Build the Future' by Peter Thiel

At the start of the millennium, a young Elon was working on X.com and found his nearest competitor to be Peter Thiel.

However, instead of brooding hostility toward him, Elon endorsed and supported his book instead and found it to be a great source of inspiration saying:

"Peter Thiel has built multiple breakthrough companies, and this book shows us how."

8. 'Superintelligence: Paths, Dangers, Strategies' by Nick Bostrom

Superintelligence gives us an insight into what the world would be like if artificial intelligence surpassed human intellect. Its discussion into computational intelligence can be terrifying at times but it's meant to be a bold and fearless portrayal of a world where humans relinquish power to computers. It would seem likely that such a book would inspire Elon as it would give him a hypothetical view on what science could create. He says:

"We need to be super careful with AI because it's potentially more dangerous than nukes."

9. 'Howard Hughes: His Life and Madness' by Donald L. Barlett and James B. Steele

Hughes and Musk certainly share some similarities. Both were visionaries who wanted to push the boundaries of technology while working across a variety of industries. Yet, although Elon cites Hughes as being one of his greatest inspirations, he doesn't want to copy him too much. Hughes famously became increasingly eccentric and in his later years and was known to have multiple phobias and lived as a recluse.

"Definitely want to make sure I don't grow my fingernails too long and start peeing in jars," says Elon. (Silver)

10. The 'Foundation' trilogy by Isaac Asimov

Being an avid sci-fi reader, Elon adores Asimov and it's easy to see why. Asimov was not only a writer but was also a professor of biochemistry and also covered subjects such as mathematics, history and astronomy. Having been known as one of the "big three" sci-fi writers of his time, he wrote over 500 books while being vice-president of Mensa.

It would be obvious to see how a young Elon would have been influenced by his work as a child as he dreamed of a future in science. The Foundation trilogy is said to be his favorite collection of Asimov's work which mirrors many historical happenings while portraying the fall of The Galactic Empire. Elon said the book taught him a great deal about history and says:

"The lessons of history would suggest that civilizations move in cycles. You can track that back quite far — the Babylonians, the Sumerians, followed by the Egyptians, the Romans, China. We're obviously in a very upward cycle right now and hopefully, that remains the case. But it may not. There could be some series of events that cause that technology level to decline. Given that this is the first time in 4.5bn years where it's been possible for humanity to extend life beyond Earth, it seems like we'd be wise to act while the window was open and not count on the fact it will be open a long time." (Wile, 2010)

11. The 'Culture' series by Iain M. Banks

Many of you might know Iain Banks for his gritty yet comedic depictions of Scottish life with books such as Espedair Street and Complicity becoming modern cult classics. However, he is also known for his science fiction work such as the Culture series. It illustrates a world created by a humanoid race that consists of aliens and artificial intelligence while being ruled by an anarchistic civilization.

Elon says it's a "compelling picture of a grand, semi-utopian galactic future. Hopefully not too optimistic about AI."

12. 'Our Final Invention' by James Barrat

While being fascinated with artificial intelligence, you might notice a theme in the books he finds most inspirational is that they also bear a warning of its dangers. As well as seeing its benefits, Elon recently said that artificial intelligence is humanity's greatest existential threat.

It should be no surprise then that he endorses a book describing the end of humanity brought on by computational intelligence. Our Final Invention looks into the future of AI and what it could mean for humanity. Barrat himself says it weighs the advantages and disadvantages while also warning of its "catastrophic downside" one you'll never hear about from Google and Apple.

13. 'The Moon Is a Harsh Mistress' by Robert Heinlein

Published in 1966, The Moon is a Harsh Mistress is a dark, dystopian tale of a group of humans exiled from Earth who set about creating a new, Libertarian society on the moon in the year 2076. It's easy to see what a fantasy lover like Elon would find attractive in this book with rebels such as a supercomputer called Mike and a one armed computer mechanic hell bent on revolution.

14. 'Merchants of Doubt' by Naomi Orestes and Erik M. Conway

This emotionally charged and highly provocative book was recommended by Elon in 2013. Written by two scientific historians who describe the connections between politics, science, and industry and how these relationships have hidden the facts behind public health problems. Musk takes this further by saying "the same people who lied about smoking are now lying about climate change."

These books shaped and inspired Musk and hopefully, they can help you to achieve your goals. Although many of them are for more analytical minds, some of them are archetypal stories that characterize the achievements of good over evil and of underdogs shaping the future through grit and determination.

WHO WERE HIS ROLE MODELS?

Whilst still in college, Musk identified three areas in which humanity would experience the greatest change; renewable energy, multi-planetary life and the internet. He then set his sights on making an impact in each area, a feat he has managed to accomplish in remarkable style.

Yet what kept him motivated and who inspired him to carry on when so many people remained skeptical of his dreams? In the same manner, books kept him eager to keep striving to make his dreams a reality, people throughout his life and history reminded him that anything is possible.

Steve Jobs

It has been said the Musk makes Steve Jobs look a child playing with an electronics kit, but whether this is true or not,

Musk has often stated Jobs as being one of his greatest inspirations. Although he also said, "everyone and their mum looks up to Steve Job".

Meanwhile, three years after Jobs' passing, it has been said that Musk is his natural successor in both the entrepreneurial and technological world. Jobs' influence can also be seen in Musk's work throughout his marketing campaigns, using similar strategies to Apple in the promotion of Tesla products. Maintaining an air of mystery, he often unveils things slowly over the course of many months giving away virtually no information. This was a strategy that Jobs often used while revealing the iPhone, one of the most successful technological products ever created.

However, the parallels between the two don't end there. They have both been dedicated to creating the most beautiful and practical designs almost to the point of obsessing over the quality. In this way, Musk can be seen to channel a great deal of Jobs' skills and aesthetic.

Jobs once said that:

"Companies fall into decline once the quality of the product becomes less important. The company starts valuing the great salesman because they're the ones who can move the needle on revenues."

And Musk has taken this into account while designing his creations. For example, you only have to watch an introduction to the 2007 iPhone to see how engaged Jobs is with the product and how immersed he is in every aspect of its design. It's almost as if he has lived and breathed its creation from the initial blueprint to its physical conception which he so proudly displays for the world to see. Musk is no different and if you watch his product introductions, you'll see him exude the same confidence, pride and familiarity that displays how personal his involvement is in his work.

There is also a striking resemblance in the way both men deal with customer service. If you're an Apple user, you might be aware of the myth that Jobs never cared for his customers. In fact, the opposite is true. Jobs cared about customer service as much as he cared for superior quality products and saw it as just important as the products themselves. He even went as far as famously phoning a disgruntled customer after lengthy delays on the repair of their computer.

Musk is no different and took inspiration from Jobs' respect for his customers. When two customers took out an ad in Palo Alto's local newspaper to give their views on Tesla's Model S, he was pleased to receive the feedback. Even when the open letter discussed ways in which the car could be improved, he paid careful consideration to each point made and responded quickly. Tweeting the ad, he agreed with the car owners' and said many of their suggestions would be immediately implemented.

Larry Page

Controversially, Page once said that when he dies, he would rather give all his money to Elon Musk rather than charity. There is much conjecture about why he said this but one thing is for certain, they are close friends and each other's inspiration.

Yet their relationship is a complicated one. They don't have relationship issues that most people have instead they disagree on various complicated scientific points. For example, Musk is wary of artificial intelligence and even donated $10m to the Future of Life Institute to research its safety. On the other hand, Larry Page wants nothing more than to advance the abilities of artificial intelligence. Musk, however, has said that he thinks Page is rather naïve about these advancements and that he could even bring about an end to humanity.

The two of them often hangout in secret in an apartment in Palo Alto to brainstorm ideas with Google co-founder, Sergey Brin (mentioned below). Some of their ideas have included a commuter plane that constantly circles the Earth and an electric jet plane that can take off and land vertically.

This unconventional friendship sees that Musk is never far away from someone to bounce ideas off and even if some of their concepts seem a little strange, there's no doubt that at least some of them will come to fruition. For example, one idea that has come into being is the Tesla Bioweapons Defense Mode which was inspired by page. Only available on the Model X, this futuristic piece of technology uses an HEPA filter to clean the car's air if you were ever unfortunate enough to be traveling through high levels of pollution or large amounts of airborne viruses. Research with the filter concluded that it could clean the air in two minutes, reducing pollution levels from 'extremely dangerous' to 'barely detectable'.

Sergey Brin

Google founders Larry Page and Sergey Brin have been close friends since meeting at Stanford University but their friendship has extended to include Musk. The powerful trio has become a formidable force in the technological world and they are often nearby to share ideas.

Musk remembers the time he took Sergey Brin for his first test drive in a Tesla electric car with Page in tow. At the time, Tesla was going under considerable changes at the time, swapping its prototype systems from analogue to digital.

Because of this, a bug seemed to be running rampant throughout the car which caused it to move no faster than 10mph. He says:

"I remember in the early days giving a test drive to Larry Page and Sergey Brin, whom I've known for a long time, and there was some, like, bug in the system, and dammit, the car would only go 10 miles an hour. And I was like Look, I swear guys it goes way faster than this." (Wile, 2010)

However, the disastrous test drive did not put off Brin and Page as they both became early investors in Tesla.

Warren Buffet

Often referred to as the "Miracle of Omaha" Warren Buffet is many people's inspiration. One of the world's greatest entrepreneurs, he exudes elegance, wealth and confidence while keeping a low profile and remaining humble and family orientated. It then comes as no surprise that Musk would look up to him for financial guidance. Unlike Jobs, Page and Brin, Buffet didn't create his great wealth through technological advancement but did so through becoming an investor and business magnate. However, there are many similarities between Musk and Buffet.

For example, they are both focused on non-carbon renewable energy with Musk being the largest shareholder in SolarCity, America's leading solar power supplier created by his cousins. Buffett's company Berkshire Hathaway Energy, on the other hand, is the largest provider of wind power in the United States being responsible for 7% of the country's wind generation.

Both also insist on remaining debt-free, finding sources of funding without leverage and both favor a specific type of funding called an insurance float. An insurance float can be quite complicated, but in essence, it means a company generates funding through receiving cash from customers that is not yet being paid out for expenses.

An example of this is that customers who want to buy a Tesla car, have to put down a $1000 deposit. When the Model 3 was unveiled in 2016, it got 373,000 ore-orders within the first month. This created a $373m cash float in which to pay for expenses. Not to mention it's interest free so think of it as a $373m loan at 0% interest. I think it's safe to say Buffet taught Musk a thing or two about funding.

Although this applies to many people, just like Buffett, Musk also focuses on the long-term and not the short-term. This accounts for both his technological plans for space exploration and investing in the stock exchange, having taken much investment inspiration from Buffett.

Finally, just like Buffett, Musk has taken the time to create his own unique brand image so that his companies are synonymous with him and his goals. However, on one hand, Buffett has a toned down, grandfatherly image, one that has made him increasingly popular and one of the richest men in the world. Musk, on the other hand, has cultivated himself as the image of a real-life Tony Stark, an eccentric scientist, inventor and genius.

Not only has Musk himself said that Buffett is a great financial inspiration, but it would seem that he has implemented many of his strategies to make Tesla, SpaceX and SolarCity the technological powerhouses that they are today.

Thomas Edison

Seen to be the greatest inventor of his time, Edison has over 1000 U.S. patents to his name and Musk is fast approaching this level of success. At the start of the 20th century, Edison set out to change the world with the lightbulb, the phonograph and the motion picture camera. Essentially, he changed the modern world forever. It would seem likely then that Musk would find him to be a motivating force in his own quest to change the modern world. And despite the fact that Tesla motors is named after Nikola Tesla, he has often stated that Edison is his favorite inventor and greatest source of inspiration. This would be surprising if it wasn't for the fact that Edison, unlike Tesla, was also an astute businessman and entrepreneur, marrying technological advancement with shrewd investing, something we can see Musk aiming for today.

Veering off into the realm of esoterica, it has also been theorized that Musk is a reincarnation of Edison himself with links between them spanning the decades. For example, Edison was nicknamed "The Wizard of Menlo Park" while Musk named one of SpaceX's rocket engines Merlin after saying:

"Being able to talk to people over long distances, to transmit images, flying, accessing vast amounts of data like an oracle. These are all things that would have been considered magic a few hundred years ago," says Musk. "So engineering is, for all intents and purposes, magic, and who wouldn't want to be a magician?" (Pritzker, 2014)

Edison may have been the Wizard of Menlo Park but it could be said the Musk is a modern wizard, manifesting the impossible through the conception of other-worldly ideas. Whether you believe in reincarnation or not, it's easy to see that Musk sought out Edison to be his main role model. Just like him, he wanted to change the world and the destiny of humanity while improving living standards and exploring the unknown world. Yet despite the similarities, there are many differences too. For example, Edison was part of the spiritualist movement, even going so far as to attempt the creation of a communication device that could speak to spirits. Elon, on the other hand, is an atheist.

Nikola Tesla

You can't mention Musk's work without thinking of Nikola Tesla, after all, Tesla Motors was named after him. So who is Nikola Tesla and what did he do? Also known as a wizard of electricity and born July 10th, 1856, he has been credited with inventing:

-The rotating electrical field

- Radar

- X rays

- Hydroelectric plants

- Cryogenic engineering

- The transistor

- The remote control

- Ball lightning

- An earthquake machine

- neon lightning

- the electric motor

- wireless communication.

Yet despite this, he died alone in poverty and is not often known for his tremendous contribution to the scientific world.

He was also close friends with Mark Twain who often accompanied him with his experiments. Tesla also never slept for more than 2 hours and once went 84 hours in his laboratory without resting. However, it was his electric motor that he is most known for today with Tesla Motor using the motor in their electric cars.

Unfortunately, this great invention was lost in amidst the chaos of the economic crisis of the time and the ensuing Second World War. We are, however, grateful that is has been resurrected in modern times so his work can be fully recognized and enjoyed to the benefit of humanity and the environment.

Winston Churchill

Musk has often cited Churchill to be one of his influences. The statesman was Prime Minster of Great Britain between the years 1940 and 1945 and again between 1951 and 1955. He was also known to be a historian, artist and won a Nobel Prize in 1953 in literature. However, he's most well-known for guiding the UK through the war and boosting morale with his spectacular speeches.

Recently, when asked by a worker on the wheel assembly line for Tesla how he coped with adversity throughout his career, Musk recited one of Churchill's most famous quotes:

"If you're going through hell, keep going."

SONGS THAT ALWAYS INSPIRE HIM

What else inspires him? Over the years he has faced struggle and adversity while trying to build his empire, looking to books and role models to help him stay motivated. And he once described starting a company as "eating glass and staring into the abyss." It's a brutal and somewhat depressing outlook on building a business. But if you're planning on saving humanity and colonizing Mars then it's no wonder you might not have the most positive outlook all the time. Especially when you're trying to juggle three global companies and five children.

Yet, he manages to keep things humorous and positive most of the time and is known to play some weird and wacky tunes from time to time to stay light-hearted.

1. "Fly Me to the Moon" -- Frank Sinatra

This might seem a little too obvious but Musk says it inspires him because: "I like the sense of possibility and it's really inspiring. And I'd really like to fly to the moon. ... You know, obviously, I own a space company, I'm going to tend to like something that involves flying to the moon. You hear this song and it sounds like it's really going to happen."

2. "Con Te Partiro" -- Andrea Bocelli

This alluring and wonderful piece of music is one of Elon's favorites. "I think that song is kind of a reminder that the world is a beautiful place. It's an incredibly beautiful song, sung really beautifully, so I think that's why it makes me feel that way about the world." (Shandrow, 2016)

3. "Santa Claus Is Coming to Town" -- Fred Astaire

This might be a surprising one, after all, we're sure Elon stopped believing in Santa Claus a long time ago. But his reasons for being drawn to it are interesting and innocent as he describes remembering it at a subconscious level. He says: "I personally don't understand it, but it's the song that I whistle the most. I don't even realize I'm whistling it. I just go into auto-whistle and this one comes up more than any other so I must like it at a subconscious level, but I'm not entirely sure why. I could guess. It's sort of a positive song. I mean, who doesn't like Santa Claus? I guess it's good to have him come to town." (Shandrow, 2016)

4. "Always Look on the Bright Side of Life" -- Monty Python

This is a common song for people looking for a quick pick-me-up and Monty Python fans. From The Life of Brian, Elon finds it uplifting and amusing because: "The characters are being crucified at the time. But I think it is a good reminder not to get focused on the negative things in life. And my personal philosophy is I'd rather be optimistic and wrong rather than pessimistic and right."

5. "America, F*ck Yeah!" -- Team America: World Police

Elon is a huge fan of South Park, Trey Parker and Matt Stone so it's no surprise that he loves Team America too. "It just captures a little bit of essence of America in both a good and a bad way."

Chapter 9 – How can he Inspire us?

We know what inspires Elon, but we also know that he inspires so many of us. So what does he say when he's trying to motivate others? And what can we learn from him if we want to follow in his footsteps?

KEEP MOVING TOWARD YOUR GOAL

There have been many moments when Elon's goal seems out of sight or that things aren't going to plan but he never gives up. In fact, he's known to say "I never ever give up. I'd either have to be incapacitated or dead to give up."

He tries to encourage you to stay focused on your goal because in the end, it's what motivates you and it never changes.

And Musk knows more than anyone how things can fail and fall apart. In 2008, it seemed almost inevitable that Tesla and SpaceX were on the brink of collapse. Telling 60 Minutes 6 years later, he said that the three failing rockets had almost crippled him and that had the 4th one failed, he would have ended up broke. Speaking candidly, he said Christmas that year was the closest he ever came to a nervous breakdown.

But where most people would have fallen apart and given up, he kept going and managed to secure funding for his ailing companies just in time for the fourth rocket to launch. Finally, when the Falcon 1 was launched, the National Aeronautics and Space Administration gave Musk a contract for $1.5 billion, ensuring SpaceX's continuation. Only a few days later, Elon was able to raise another $50 million dollars proving that, although he was working against the odds, he kept his goal in mind and never doubted himself.

"When something is important enough, you do it even if the odds are not in your favor."

YOUR PRODUCTS MATTER THE MOST

It might seem obvious but quality can often fall by the wayside when companies have to tighten their purse strings. However, this is not something that Elon sees as an option and his products have become as iconic as he has. As a perfectionist, he sees that everything he does is to the best of his ability while ensuring everyone keeps up to strive for the best. And it's this relentless perfectionism that has seen his companies grow from strength to strength while keeping a loyal customer base.

ALWAYS BE PREPARED TO LEARN

One of the most impressive things about Elon is that he is an entirely self-taught computer programmer as well as teaching himself physics and even rocket science! It just goes to show that anything is possible if you're willing to work hard and push your limits.

HAVE A RELENTLESS WORK ETHIC

Musk considers himself a workaholic and just like other billionaires such as Mark Zuckerberg, he can be seen working up to 18 hours a day. Often seen working at least 100 hours a week, Elon says he only sleeps for a maximum 6 hours a night and remains alert and motivated with caffeine. And he manages to maintain this while fathering five children and having a social life! What makes this work for Elon is that he loves his job and doesn't want to do anything else. He pursues his passions and gives it his all, encouraging his employees to do the same. This means that there's less of a chance he'll burn himself out as he'll be reveling in every second of his working day.

DON'T PUT ALL YOUR EGGS IN ONE BASKET

With such a diverse portfolio, Elon makes sure he spreads his interests across many different areas from rocket science to finance, cars and interplanetary travel. From Paypal to Zip2, SpaceX and Tesla Motors, he's influenced the world in seismic ways and shown that entrepreneurial variety can be extremely rewarding.

BE READY TO MAKE SOME SACRIFICES

It's easy to see that Musk gives every business venture his all, investing everything he has even when there's a risk of going broke. He's not afraid of making tough decisions, even if the right thing to do to reach your goal is the scariest thing. A lesson we can all learn from Elon is that when you really believe what you do, don't hold back and don't be afraid to make sacrifices if it can help you achieve your dreams.

DON'T GET EASILY OFFENDED AND LEARN THAT ALL FEEDBACK IS GOOD

Elon doesn't feel insulted by critics who have a thing or two to say about him and his products. Instead, he tries to open up a dialogue with them while keeping a cool head. He knows that any feedback is good feedback and that you can learn from your mistakes. He's constantly assessing what he's doing and how it could be better and he' s not afraid to admit when he's made a mistake, seeing every failure as an opportunity to learn something new.

HE'S NOT AFRAID TO GET HIS HANDS DIRTY

Elon might be the guy with the big ideas, but he knows how to implement them on a practical level too. Being an accomplished engineer, he knows the ins and outs of his projects at a 'hands on' level and is always eager to get stuck in. This is what sets him apart from other entrepreneurs. It's rare to see most billionaires on the assembly line but this is exactly where he wants to be. You'll also find him test driving his own cars, not wanting to delegate the important tasks to someone else. For him, it's all about the details and he wants to make sure every single aspect of his product is perfect for his customers. What we can learn from Elon is that it pays to be practical. He's less interested in boardroom meetings than he is in standing shoulder to shoulder with his junior level workers. This makes him a great leader within his companies, and someone you can give directions while also being approachable.

ONLY THE BEST WILL DO

When Elon wants a project done he doesn't hire just anybody. He brings the most brilliant minds in the world together and sets tough goals. Elon is famous for making his employees work at an intense level, but this is what gets him results. He puts everything into this work and won't settle for anything less, making sure that his staff are just as dedicated as him.

THERE'S NO SUCH THING AS TOO MUCH AMBITION

There's no doubt that Elon is motivated and ambitious, but his drive for success is like no other. Even when the odds are stacked against him and it looks as though he's destined for certain failure, he still perseveres, driven by the aching feeling that he's doing the right thing, not just for him and his business, but for mankind. Even after three failed rocket launches, he continued with the fourth, even though he was strongly advised not to do so. Just like his predecessors such as Steve Jobs, Nikola Tesla and Thomas Edison, he's never too tired or defeated to try just one more time.

Chapter 10 – Personal Life

JUSTINE

While being worth over $12 billion, you'd think that he'd be quite the catch, but a steady romantic life hasn't come easy for him. As a youngster, his shyness often held him back from talking to girls so it wasn't until he reached his college years that he developed more confidence.

It was at Queen's University in Ontario that he first met Justine. At the time she was an aspiring writer from a small town in her first year. Recovering from a messy breakup with an older man, she liked the quintessential bad boy and especially loved the idea of forbidden love. She says:

"I liked poetic and rebellious and tortured. I liked a guy who parked his motorcycle beneath my dorm-room window and called my name through the twilight: Romeo in a dark-brown leather jacket." (Greenfield, 2010) Of course, this could not be further away from what Elon was at this time. Justine, in an interview for Marie Claire, remembers him as being clean-cut, upper class and smart with a strong South African accent. He says he just appeared in front of her one day as she was stepping out of her dorm and said he remembered her from a party she was certain she'd never been to. Of course, it would take many years for him to confess that he'd actually spotted her across a room and decided he wanted to talk to her.

Inviting a reluctant Justine out for ice cream, she initially said yes, then changed her mind. Leaving a note on her bedroom door, she tried to politely turn him down. A few hours later, with her head bent over her Spanish textbook in the library, she turned around to see a smiling Elon with two chocolate ice cream cones in his hands as they melted and dripped down over his fingers. She knew right then that he never took no for an answer.

However, Justine became quickly aware that she was not the only woman he was pursuing at the time. Deciding to keep a cool distance, she tried to not get too involved but even when he was transferred to another college, he continued to woo her by sending roses. So when he arrived back at Queen's and invited her out for dinner, she naturally said yes.

That night, as they perused through the shelves of a local bookstore, Justine pointed to an empty space and said:

"I want my books to go right there."

She knew she was taking a gamble when she said this as she remembered previously telling a close friend the same thing only to be laughed at. However, she was pleased to see that Elon took her seriously. In fact, he seemed impressed and she was smitten with the idea that he found her ambition attractive unlike previous boyfriends who were more focused on her "long hair and narrow waist".

Justine complained that boys often found her too competitive to be with and found her drive for literary success off putting. Elon, on the contrary, said that he liked the "fire in her soul" and that he saw a lot of himself in her.

Yet despite them getting along well, it would seem that events would overtake their romance and they found themselves going in separate directions. Justine, after graduation, moved to Japan where she taught English studies. She then returned a year later to take on a bartending job and work on her first novel. She also needed to decide if going to grad school was the right thing to do or whether she should return to Japan. However, she found herself thinking of Elon at this time and she remembers telling her sister:

"If Elon ever calls me again, I think I'll go for it. I might have missed something there."

It would certainly seem that it was it was meant to be when only a week later, Elon called and she took her chance.

At the time he was living in Silicon Valley with three of his friends as he started up Zip2, and she flew out to meet him. She fondly remembers him taking her out to dinner and asking her how many children she'd like to have. She replied she'd like to have one or two but if she was able to afford a nanny she'd like four. Elon replied "That's the difference between you and me. I always assumed I'd be able to afford nannies." He then went on to make a rocking motion with his arms before whispering "Baby..."

After this, he took her to a nearby book shop and presented her with his credit card telling her to buy as much as she wanted. As she recalls this memory, she says: "No man could have said anything sweeter."

While dating the twenty something entrepreneur, she found his snowballing wealth to be something that made her uncomfortable. Gone were the days when he was just another struggling internet kid with a start-up. He was now a serious contender in the tech world and she often found his skyrocketing career to be intimidating.

"Elon's wealth seemed abstract and unreal, a string of zeros that existed in some strange space of its own. I made uneasy jokes that he was about to dump me for a supermodel."

However, luckily for Justine, he did no such thing and one day as they were taking a walk, he got down on one knee on a street corner and proposed.

Suddenly, she found herself to be living with a millionaire as Elon's worth grew to $20 million. But now they were engaged, he took the time and money to renovate an 1800 sq ft condo to give Justine a luxurious home. It was also around this time that he bought his Mclaren F1, and a small plane. Yet, despite the newfound wealth, she says that everyday life was ordinary for them with the only extraordinary thing being the occurrence of weekly flying lessons.

However, although Justine assumed that she was about to marry her soulmate, there were early signs that things might not be working out. She remembers being taken by Elon to an attorney to sign a financial agreement. As she sat at the desk and looked down at the document, she felt a hint of anxiety and looked up to him. He quickly blurted out: "Don't worry, it's not a pre-nup" but this did little to assuage her nerves.

Talking about this incident now, she says she never realized that Elon was bringing her into a state of "mediation", meaning anything said in confidence can be used in a court of law. Finding the whole situation confusing, she now regrets not know the ins and outs of the process and says "I had no time to research mediation, or learn that it rarely serves the interest of the less powerful person in the relationship."

There were other warning signs too. On the day of the wedding, she was enjoying the best day of her life until the first dance. She says Elon pulled her close and whispered in her ear "I'm the alpha in this relationship." Although this seemed odd, she didn't dwell on it and was still convinced that she was marrying her soul mate, the man she loved and trusted. And speaking about her love for him all these years later, she still remembers those halcyon days fondly.

She recalls a time shortly before he proposed when they were both napping in the spring time sun before getting ready to attend a friend's wedding. Her arm was wrapped around him and she suddenly had the realization that life without him was utterly unthinkable. As she watched him sleep with her arm draped over his chest, she felt that he was her own private Alexander the Great.

However, after the wedding, the warning signs continued. Two months into their marriage, he asked her to sign a pre-nup, something she hadn't the least bit of desire in doing. But she did it anyway and though little of it at the time. After all, she trusted him and never for a moment thought they would get divorced.

It wasn't until they were married for quite some time that she realized Elon was deadly serious about a lot of the things she had often jokingly shrugged off. She speaks of his life growing up in a patriarchal South African home where you were expected to compete and be the best at everything. And although this ambitious spark has made Elon what he is today, it did not bode well for his relationships with Justine.

"The will to compete and dominate that made him so successful in business did not magically shut off when he came home," she says.

And there was more to come. As Elon's career and wealth continued to escalate at a rapid rate, Justine's did not. Soon, a seismic rift started to form between the two as a financial and emotional imbalance began to threaten the marriage. Justine remembers this as a time when a power struggle between the two began to form and Elon decided he was the boss of the marriage. He was always finding areas in which she was lacking and she'd often have to remind him that she was his wife, not his employee. To which he always replied, "If you were an employee I would fire you."

Despite this, Justine was eager to make the marriage work and by 2002 they had moved to Los Angeles and were expecting their first child. It wasn't long until baby Nevada Alexander was born and it seemed as though life was on track.

Ten weeks later, Paypal was bought over by Ebay which sent Elon's fortune being catapulted to over $100 million. The same week, Justine put baby Nevada down in his crib for an afternoon nap. When she returned, she found that he wasn't breathing. Although emergency services were called immediately, he had been starved of oxygen for so long that he was clinically brain dead. Three heart breaking days passed with Nevada on life support before it was decided there was nothing that could be done for him. The life support was shut off and Nevada died in Justine's arms.

It was discovered that their little boy had died of SIDS – sudden infant death syndrome. Justine and Elon had to come to terms with the fact that there was nothing they could have done to save their son.

It was around this time that the cracks in their relationship started to become more obvious. Justine wanted to grieve openly, she wanted to seek comfort from her husband and talk about the loss of their son. But Elon didn't want to say a word about him, choosing to keep his grief to himself. This was something that became a bone of contention between the two with Elon saying Justine's crying and grief was "emotionally manipulative." Because of this, Justine was forced to keep her feelings secret and so life went on.

Only two months passed after the death of Nevada when Elon and Justine decided they should try for another baby. It was a way for them both to cope with their son's death and so Justine found herself undergoing IVF, a procedure that saw her having twins and then triplets two years later.

Although she now had her hands full with her children, the grief and memory of Nevada still swamped her and she found herself struggling. Even when her literary career took off and she sold three novels to Penguin and Simon and Schuster, nothing took the pain away. Luckily for Justine, her nanny noticed that she was struggling and after a year-long bout of severe depression, she gave her the number of a therapist she knew. At first, Justine was skeptical and couldn't see how a therapist could make the grief go away. But with nothing to lose, she began weekly sessions, something she remembers now as a time when she started to gain perspective on her life.

Life, it would seem, was back on track. Now in their 6000 sq ft mansion in Bel Air, they had everything they could ever want. And by the time they were married for seven years they were living in a house that Justine thinks of today as a workplace. With domestic staff and constant fund raisers, it would seem that they were deeply entrenched in Elon's millionaire fantasy, something that was reiterated by their celebrity parties. Justine remembers those days as being a heady mix of glamor and luxurious travel.

"When Google cofounder Larry Page got married on Richard Branson's private Caribbean island, we were there, hanging out in a villa with John Cusack and watching Bono pose with swarms of adoring women outside the reception tent. When we traveled, we drove onto the airfield up to Elon's private jet, where a private flight attendant handed us champagne. I spent an afternoon walking around San Jose with Daryl Hannah, where she caused a commotion at Starbucks when the barista asked her name and she said, blithely, "Daryl.""

For Justine, it was a glittery dream, the best times of her life but also the most unreal. However, the money, celebrity friends and prestigious parties couldn't hide the fact that a rift was once again beginning to form between Elon and Justine, one that this time might be impossible to heal over.

She recalls it as a time when Elon was so obsessed with his work that little else mattered, especially her. She longed for the intimacy that comes from a happy marriage and to do normal things that couples take for granted iike spend time together and have an in depth, heart-fell conversation. More than anything she wanted to feel as though she was married to Elon and that deep down he had some compassion and empathy for her. But it wasn't to be. She describes him as being a man who would be at home while his mind was at work.

She would often try to explain the complexities of her life and the importance of her book deadlines. She'd often try to tell him about the sacrifices the family made for the greater good of his work but he would often shrug off her concerns and dismiss them by insinuating that she "read too much" into his actions. Soon the couple were constantly arguing and mundane tasks like putting the children to bed became battlegrounds in which an exhausted Justine would find her flaws and weaknesses scrutinized. It was at this point that she says she began to feel insignificant, a feeling that worried her because she was concerned about the message Elon and her behaviour was sending to their five young sons.

It would seem the couple were at breaking point. Was it that Justine felt that her needs were being ignored? Or was it that Elon simply thought his race to colonize Mars a superior use of his time than the trivialities of family life? Or was it neither? Were they simply a couple who fell out of love like so many others?

No matter which side you look at things, it would seem that the couple were now reaching breaking point, and Justine's sudden awareness of the end of things came in the physical manifestation of a car crash. It was life changing and horrifying and something that she remembers in vivid detail to this day. She remembers the look of terror on the other driver's face as she ploughed into the front of her car, she remembers the cell phone held to her ear and the crunch of the metal as the vehicles collided. She was aware of the space between them as the distance narrowed and they were now moulded together in a tangled mess of twisted metal and broken glass. And she remembers the gut wrenching feeling that swept over her as she realized what had happened. "When we skidded to a halt, my first thought wasn't, Thank God nobody's hurt. It was, My husband, is going to kill me!"

Suddenly, she saw herself as if for the first time and noticing all the changes that had taken place within both her body and mind. She realized how thin and blonde she was, how tired and injured. She was aware of how expensive the car was as she looked at the way the front wheel arch bended in on itself. She was finally aware that she was a trophy wife and she "sucked at it".

She realized that she wasn't all the things that were expected of her. She wasn't interested in makeup or plastic surgery. She didn't agree that men should do all the talking while women simply looked pretty, nodded and smiled.

Justine found herself wanting to be back at the start of their relationship before they were married, a time when all either of them wanted was to be loved and respected. Despite all the years of being married to a multi-millionaire and having every material need met, she found that she was not equal, nor was she a partner in the marriage. Feeling as though she was a sidekick in Elon's master plan, she confronted after the accident and told him that their life needed to change.

Agreeing to make things work, the couple began counselling but after three sessions it was evident it wasn't going to work. The end of the third session resulted in a row in which Elon gave her an ultimatum, she get behind him or she get out. The next morning he filed for divorce.

Although heart breaking, she describes this as a moment of feeling tremendously numb while simultaneously being relieved. However, the breakup may have been swift but the divorce certainly wasn't. After two years of legal wrangling, the couple ended up in court over their finances where the judge ruled in Elon's favour before the case was appealed.

Justine is now estranged from Elon and shares joint custody of the children and, against the odds she also went on to become close friends with Elon's next wife, Talulah Riley. She never expected to like her, for obvious reasons. And she often laughed that friends were confused as to why she didn't want to "poke chopsticks in her eyeballs" but Justine only has good things to say about the woman:

"She is ... better fitted to my ex-husband's lifestyle and personality than I ever was. Although she had dark hair when she and Elon first met, she is now blonder than I've ever been."

Elon himself is not the biggest fan of disclosing private information, choosing to stick to his work that discussing matters of the heart in public. He says: "Given the choice, I'd rather stick a fork in my hand than write about my personal life." (Wile, 2010)

However, he has had to clarify many aspects of the messy divorce which he thought were misrepresented in the media, citing enormous legal fees causing his financial demise. In California, the wealthier spouse is legally obligated to pay legal fees on both sides, even if they are not the one inciting the divorce. This meant that Elon was paying an estimated $174'000 a month for 24 months!

And there are more discrepancies between him and his wife as he states: "My ex-wife also contributes frequently to the public literature on the divorce ... contributing several more inaccuracies that I would like to correct."

We may never know the full story about the divorce and or what took place within the marriage. Although we do know that both Justine and Elon were quick to move on from one another. Justine later became engaged to a long-term friend of the couple, Matt Peterson while Elon, not long after his divorce, met young actress Talulah Riley.

TALULAH RILEY

Moving on from Justine was a quick process for Elon and just six weeks after he filed for divorce, he texted his ex-wife to say he was engaged to a British actress in her twenties and that she had moved to Los Angeles to be with him.

Born in Hemel Hempstead, the young actress attended two of Britain's most prestigious and expensive private schools - Cheltenham Ladies College and Haberdashers' Aske's School for Girls. She later went on to appear in St Trinian's, Inception, Thor and Westworld. While acting she studied for her degree in Natural Sciences with the Open University.

However, Elon's hastiness to begin a new romance with a girl much younger than the mother of his children saw him being heavily criticized. But in an article he wrote for Business Insider, he was eager to defend himself and put the record straight.

"It is worth mentioning that Talulah, as anyone who knows her would attest, is one of the most kind hearted and gentle people in the world. The cliché that has been propagated, of me abandoning a devoted wife to "run off" with a young actress, could not have been more falsely applied."

So how did the new couple meet? It's not often that young actresses find themselves in the company of tech superstars. Talulah remembers the night vividly. She had been to a gala before joining some friends in the Whisky Mist club in Mayfair. Musk remembers seeing her and thinking she looked like Cinderella and Talulah recalls his nervousness to be introduced to her. He was shy and reserved and she says: "I remember thinking this guy probably didn't get to talk to young actresses a lot and seemed quite nervous."

As the two began to talk, Elon blurted out that he'd like to show her his rocket. Thinking this to be some vulgar euphemism, Talulah laughed. But then he proceeded to pull out his phone and actually show her video footage of his rockets, something that shocked and dazzled her.

At the time she was only twenty two and a virgin but she was excited to meet him despite not knowing a single thing about his work. Elon was also apprehensive to tell her about his ongoing divorce with Justine or his five sons. So it wasn't until Talulah's father, Doug Milburn, who also happens to be the former head of the National Crime Squad, did some research on him that she discovered who he really was.

Agreeing to go on a date with him, she met him the next day to visit an art gallery before venturing back to Elon's hotel room. And it wasn't long until the couple were officially together. A few weeks later, as they lay in bed in his Los Angeles home, he asked her to marry him. Then he apologized because he didn't have a ring. They sealed the deal with a handshake and two years later they were married. In 2014, they wed at Dornoch Cathedral in the Scottish Highlands.

However, it wasn't to be the perfect relationship and Talulah remember a lot of turmoil in those early days. At the time, both Tesla and SpaceX were on the cusp of collapsing and Elon, despite his fortune on paper, was finding himself deeper and deeper in financial difficulties. And despite being known as a billionaire, he was funding his work projects with loans he'd acquired from friends and investors. At one point, he was in so much trouble Talulah's parents even offered to re-mortgage their home in order to help him pay his workers' wages.

It didn't help the relationship that Elon is a serious workaholic, something that has propelled him to great success but has left him bereft of a normal family life. His official biographer, Ashlee Vance says his constant drive for perfection has created a sense of inner turmoil as he struggles to balance his work and family. And the rift beginning to form between Elon and Talulah only grew the more he worked. Putting in up to 18 hours a day between his various business ventures and spending Sundays at his rocket factory, it would seem he had little time to spare for his new wife, no matter how much he loved her.

Vance recalls talking to him about his marriage and him asking: "How much time does a woman want per week? Ten hours minimum?" She thought it to be a typical thing for Elon to ask as, just like his work, he thought marriage and love could be technically analysed and quantified.

Always the hard worker, Elon had only ever taken two weeks off from work, an experience that he hated. After a holiday to Brazil in 2002, he came down with a bout of malaria and remembering it some years later, he said: "That's my lesson for taking a vacation. It will kill you."

Meanwhile, his marriage to Talulah was starting to show cracks. Being so preoccupied with his work, he forgot to buy her a present for their first Christmas together, and in desperate need of a gift, he rushed into a nearby shop and bought her a plastic monkey ornament.

Shortly after this, the pressure and stress of his work piled up on him and he retreated from public life, lost weight and suffered terrible nightmares. Talulah remembers this time:

"He looked like death itself. He was in physical pain. He would climb on me and start screaming while still asleep."

But no matter how much stress he was suffering or how ill he was, failure was not an option and he was more eager than ever to see his dreams at SpaceX and Tesla come to fruition. This went as far as him being so impatient with his employees that he would often do their work for them at night because things weren't progressing as fast as he wanted them to.

This often gave the impression that he was a harsh and unforgiving boss. Around this time one of his aides, a woman who had worked for him for over ten years, asked for a pay rise. His response was that he would give her two weeks holiday in which he would take on her job to gauge the level of difficulty of her duties. When the two weeks were over he fired her.

It would seem that his perfectionism had no limit and he wanted all his employees to be just as dedicated as he was. One of his employees remembers being told: "I want you to think ahead and think so hard every day that your head hurts. I want your head to hurt every night when you go to bed."

In 2012, Talulah, unable to cope with the ups and downs of their relationship, filed for divorce. This saw her walking away with a $16 million settlement. At the time, he said:

"It was an amazing four years. I will love you forever. You will make someone very happy one day."

But the couple, who still to this day remain best friends, remarried in the summer of 2014, only for Talulah to file for divorce six months later. In an interview with The Times, she said:

'We really are best friends. I'll always love him, I'll always be there for him.'

Journalist Stephanie Marsh said she thought that would be the perfect basis for a marriage, to which Talulah laughed and replied: "You'd think."

When asked if she'd marry him for the third time she said "Never say never. When you've been with someone for eight years on and off, you really learn how to love them. He and I are very good at loving each other".

They did marry for the third time in 2013 but then split up once again with their divorce being finalized in October 2016.

AMBER HEARD

Musk met Amber while performing a cameo role in Machete Kills in 2013 and it has been said that he immediately became infatuated with her. Although neither of them appeared on set together and had no chance to officially meet, he was eager to see her and constantly emailed director Robert Rodrigues to introduce him. This was despite the fact that she was married to Johnny Depp at the time. He wrote: 'If there is a party or event with Amber, I'd be interested in meeting her just out of curiosity. Allegedly, she is a fan of George Orwell and Ayn Rand ... most unusual. If there is a party or event with Amber, I'd be interested in meeting her just out of curiosity." (Cappuccino, 2016)

No doubt her love for literature set her apart from other actresses while she also maintained Elon's ideal female image; thin blonde and beautiful.

After receiving repeated emails, Rodriguez finally set up a dinner for the both of them but Amber refused to turn up. Never easily deterred and known for not taking no for an answer, Elon asked if she could meet him for lunch in LA. Although he made sure to clarify his intentions.

"I'm not angling for a date. I know she's in a long-term relationship, but … Amber just seems like an interesting person to meet."

Since then they have been seen numerous times together although Elon insists they are just friends. Despite this, friends of Amber have said she is smitten with the billionaire.

Chapter 11: Private Thoughts

POLITICAL STANCE

Elon is famously as enigmatic about his political opinion as he is about his work. Although he describes himself as being "nauseatingly pro-America" he doesn't give much away about which side he supports. To make things more confusing, he often donates equal amounts of money to both the Republican and Democratic campaigns.

However, his support for the United States is unwavering and says it is unarguably the greatest country that has ever existed on Earth. He says it is "the greatest force for good of any country that's ever been" and that democracy would not exist were it not for America. In fact, he thinks twentieth century democracy would have been obliterated if the United States was not in place to prevent further disastrous consequences in WWI, WWII, and The Cold War.

Just like with his personal life, he notoriously shies away from disclosing his political opinion and the only time he is known to do so publicly, landed him in hot water. In 2013 shortly after the death of former British Prime Minster, Margaret Thatcher, he tweeted: "Always admired Margaret Thatcher — she was tough but sensible & fair, much like my English Nana."

Immediately after this, Twitter went into overdrive with people enraged and he was on the receiving end of criticism. In response, he said there were no political opinions from him again after he'd "shot off both his feet."

RELIGION

He might be guarded about politics but he's definitely let his opinion on life and the universe well-known stating it's not likely that religion and science can co-exist in harmony. When asked if he believed in a destiny that surpassed physics, he said:

"Well, I do. Do I think that there's some sort of master intelligence architecting all of this stuff? I think probably not because then you have to say: "Where does the master intelligence come from?" So it sort of begs the question. So I think really you can explain this with the fundamental laws of physics. You know its complex phenomenon from simple elements."

He has said that he does not pray to an entity or worship any being at all, however, at the launch of the Falcon 1, he did ask that if any entity at all was watching, please could they bless the launch.

But he takes this further. He hit the headlines recently by discussing the possibility that we're not here at all and that life, the universe, and everything in it is actually a simulation. It's a terrifying thought and one that was no received well. But what exactly was he talking about?

The simulation hypothesis theory presents three cases in which one must be true:

1. Everything we know to be real is a computer simulation

2. In the future, advanced civilizations will be opposed to making "ancestor civilizations."

3. Something will destroy all civilization before the technological capability is met in which to simulate consciousness.

If this seems mind-bending to you then you are not alone. Many people have refused to get behind Elon's idea that we are all the product of a grand cyber architect in the sky. However,

Elon is so sure of this possibility that he says there is only a 1 in a billion chance that we are not a simulation. So why does he think this? He explains it as:

"The strongest argument for us being in a simulation is the following: 40 years ago, we had pong, two rectangles and a dot. That is what games were. Now 40 years later we have photorealistic 3D simulations with millions of people playing simultaneously and it's getting better every year. And soon we'll have virtual reality, augmented reality, if you assume any rate of improvement at all, the games will become indistinguishable from reality." (New God Argument)

Parenting

In a world where every part of Musk's life is scrutinized, you would not be surprised to learn that his unorthodox way of raising his children has come under fire. Whether it's from his constant multi-tasking which sees him send emails and taking business calls while his children are on his lap, or whether it's keeping his five sons out of mainstream school. It would seem that everyone has an opinion. But what is so different about Musk's parenting and why are people so fascinated with it?

In a community where children have the best, Musk makes sure that his children really do have everything he can give them. One of the things he has done for them is build them their very own school, Ad Astra which translates as 'to the stars'. There isn't a great deal known about it. There's no website or application process and no one even knows exactly where it is. All that is known is that it is located somewhere in Southern California and only has 14 pupils, although there is a plan to extend that to 20 in the next year.

Being one of the most exclusive schools in the world, we can only wonder who the pupils are and how they were allowed access to such a secretive and prestigious establishment. There is some speculation that the pupils are the children of fellow SpaceX employees, however this has never been confirmed.

While planning his children's education, Musk didn't want his sons to be confined by the trivialities of mainstream school. He wanted them to think on their feet and learn actively through a process of problem solving. This is opposed to the passive method of staring at a blackboard and merely taking notes.

And his main goal was to really integrate the children into practical and academic work. He says if you'd want to teach a child how an engine works, you wouldn't present them first with a hammer and a wrench etc... You would surely show them the engine and then the use for the hammer and wrench would become apparent.

So who are the teachers at Ad Astra? Well we do know that the first teacher was brought from Los Angeles' Mirman School. Mirman is also an exclusive school and only accepts the most gifted of children. In fact, potential pupils have to take an IQ test during the application process and there is no regular grading system.

Speak on Chinese television, he explains that he was inspired to build his own school because his own experiences were so terrible. He described his school days as being torture, a place that he absolutely hated. He also felt that regular schools and the modern teaching paradigm didn't do what he hoped they would.

In a way, Musk is rebelling against that paradigm. As a child, he often didn't fit in at school and found the timetabled, highly structured learning process to be a hindrance. So much so that he often got terrible grades in his most beloved subjects like maths and physics.

Yet this is the opposite of what his children have today. He jokes that they love school so much that they think vacations are too long. "They can't wait to get back to school!"

It would seem that he's figured out the perfect solution to teaching by learning the hard way through his own experiences. But of course, he does think there is a downside to Ad Astra and the privileges his children have. Although he is pleased that his children don't have to suffer like he did as a child, he feels that in a way they are missing out on the experience of adversity. This is something that he feels gave him great strength and will and made him who he is today. Yet this is a common concern of the rich and famous. If a child is born with the very best then what do they have to aspire to?

Alongside this, Musk shares many of the same problems that many other parents face. He says the main battle he faces with his children is cutting down on their screen time. As they're all eager gamers like him, he complains that they want to play "all the time." Although he's figured out the solution to this problem too. "The rule is they have to read more than play video games." (Silver)

He also uses his children's love of video games to teach them and he always makes sure they don't play games that don't challenge them. "They also can't play completely stupid video games. There's one game they downloaded called 'Cookies' or something. You literally tap a fucking cookie. It's like a psych 101 experiment. I made them delete the cookie game. They had to play flappy golf instead, which is like flappy bird, but at least there are some physics involved."

Lastly, despite all the turmoil in his life, the intense work regime and the long hours. Despite living his life in the limelight and trying to launch all of mankind to another planet to save us all. Despite having a busier life than any of us can imagine, he always makes sure he has time for his children. No matter what happens, he's home to have dinner with them and puts time aside to play video games. At a recent conference, he was eager to tell the audience what he thought about children.

"Kids are awesome, you guys should all have kids. Kids are great."

Chapter 12: An Uncertain Future

The sheer number of plates Elon Musk keeps spinning at any given time is impressive to anyone on the outside looking in. While this has, throughout his life, translated to impressive returns, both in the financial sense and in his ultimate goal to move human progress forward, there have recently been questions raised about whether Musk can keep up this pace as he moves into the future—or whether he's finally reached a point where his reach exceeds his unquestionably incredible abilities.

Musk's two major companies at the start of 2016 were Tesla Motors and SpaceX. Though he is not an official member of the staff of SolarCity, he is made a significant financial investment in that company, as well. For years, there have been questions surrounding the true profitability of Musk's advanced technology work. Many people have accused him of making unrealistic promises and fudging the true financial success rate of all his companies. The fact is that SolarCity has yet to turn a true profit in any quarter of its existence—not an especially unusual situation for a business model that relies on turning many profits back into the company, but perhaps alarming from trying to make solar power a more wide-spread sustainable energy option. Since SpaceX is not publically traded, there's no way to know for sure whether the company has ever been profitable or not. This, too, has raised some eyebrows around the tech company world, from people who are starting to wonder if Elon Musk is truly as successful as people have credited him with being.

What can't be denied, of course, are Musk's technological developments. His projects in the first half of 2016 included the first successful vertical landing of a launching system ever in the history of space travel; the unveiling and remarkable pre-sale of Tesla Motors' newest vehicle, the Model 3; the first tests of his Hyperloop technology by Hyperloop One; and the launch of OpenAI's first publically available program—not a bad list of accomplishments even for someone who's so consistently prolific as Elon Musk. Still, that laundry list is in no way a guarantee of financial growth, and other factors that have transpired over the first half of 2016 have left many analysts wondering just how long Musk can sustain his various attempts at revolutionizing humanity.

Financial losses

The fourth quarter of 2015 dealt a crushing blow to both SolarCity and Tesla Motors—Musk's two largest current investments besides his private company, SpaceX. This was an ugly quarter for many stocks, but the performance of these two companies was especially bad. Between December 31, 2015, and February 10, 2016, shares of Tesla Motors stock dropped a staggering 40%. This resulted in a total loss of around $12 billion to the company's investors. Being the primary shareholder in the company, Musk personally lost around $2.8 billion from this drop in stock prices—his total stake in Tesla even after this loss is around $4.2 billion.

This drop in Tesla Motors stocks comes after four straight quarterly losses from the company and has been especially disappointing to investors, who believed their stocks were on the verge of turning around and going back to making a profit at the end of 2015. This large drop was in part due to the advice was given by Citron Research, a major stock trader advising company. Citron revealed to the public that Tesla Motors has been having significant issues on both the supply side and the demand side of their newest vehicle, the Model X crossover

SUV. Supply issues prevented the company from making as many of the cars as they initially had hoped and planned. Citron advised its readers to "short" Tesla's stock and predicted that the stock could fall to $100 by the end of the year—a 46% drop from its current stock price.

This is not the first time Citron has warned investors to stay away from Tesla. In August of 2013, Citron released a lengthy explanation of why smart investors should steer clear of Tesla Motors, saying that it would not be able to generate a large enough following among the price-sensitive mass market consumer base once it had filled orders from early adopters and "high net worth trendsetters."

They argued that most car buyers be more concerned with how many dollars they are paying per month than the question of emerging technology. Citron's advice at that point was largely misguided; Tesla Motors stock gained nearly 400% between 2013 and 2016, a much greater increase than is traditionally seen in the stocks of automakers. Still, with investors by and large shying away from risky stocks and caring more about profits than innovation, it is advice that will no doubt continue to impact the performance of Tesla Motors on the public exchange. In early February 2016, Tesla's stock hit its lowest level in two years.

Though Musk's stock in SolarCity is not as large—meaning his personal losses from the company were not as great—the company's stock performance as a whole was in even worse shape when fourth quarter results from 2015 were released on February 10, 2016. The company announced that shares were likely to lose around $2.65 in the coming quarter, an even deeper loss than most investors were expecting. As a result, the stock dropped 29%, down to $18.63 per share, by the end of trading on February 10. This brings the total losses for 2016 to 48%.

Part of this drop was fueled by announcements that SolarCity ended its operations in Nevada following a decision by the Nevada Public Utilities Commission to cut subsidies for solar customers in December of 2015.

Like Tesla Motors, SolarCity is a company that's high on valuation but thin on profit. Both companies have always been a risky proposition for investors, but one many were willing to take based largely on their knowledge of Musk's previous investment prowess. The continuous stacking up of losses for the companies has started making their investors question the wisdom of following Musk's lead in recent months, however, for his part, Musk has seen a total of $3.5 billion in losses between his holdings on Tesla and SolarCity; the total loss for all investors in the same span of time was around $15.7 billion. Since the fall-off in mid-February, Tesla's stock has started to improve, and rose 30% in the months following the drop, but will need to make even greater strides in the coming quarters if the company hopes to win back investor trust.

Problems with the products themselves have also impacted the growth of Musk's businesses. An April 2016 recall went out on all Model X cars that had been sold in the United States, designed to fix a faulty locking hinge in the SUV's second- and third-row seats. The fault increases the risk that these seats will fall forward if there's crash. The recall is based on results from an E.U. safety test, which put more stringent requirements on the car than those imposed by the U.S. test, thus explaining why the cars were able to go out to customers in the first place. The recall is not serious, and costs for the fixes will be paid by the original supplier of the seats, but it is nonetheless another black mark on a company that has lost much of its favor with investors in recent months.

Industry changes

The drop in oil prices worldwide is the worst thing that can happen for Elon Musk's major industries. Falling oil prices reduce the sense of urgency and enthusiasm that surrounded electric cars and solar power in the early years of the decade. For those, like Musk, who are ideologically connected to the idea of alternative energy sources, the drop in gas prices is a terrible thing for the future of humanity. It means people are willing to buy gas-guzzling cars and aren't concerned with switching to more efficient vehicles and means of gaining power. Cheap gas delays the transformation to sustainable energy that could combat global warming—as Musk says, "weakening the economic-forcing function to sustainable transport and clean energy in general." Musk has called for consumers to fight fossil fuel industry propaganda and think of the future, not simply their pocketbooks, but this is arguably an easier task for someone whose pockets are as deep as Musk's than it is for the average middle-class American.

Due to issues with suppliers and pushed back release dates on Tesla Motors' newest model, Musk is also in the uncomfortable situation of having been the innovator of electric car technology—and now finding that his company will likely not be the first to make an affordable plug-in car available to the mass market. GM will be releasing its Bolt in late 2016, a plug-in vehicle that's expected to cost around $30,000. The Model 3 is supposed to come out in 2017, but many analysts believe its actual release will not occur until 2018, based on Musk's history of making optimistic assumptions about the release dates of his new products.

Of course, this particular financial setback must elicit mixed emotions in Musk. He has long been committed to keeping his technology open-source and has stated that his goal for Tesla

Motors is to increase the availability of electric cars for the mass market consumer. Though he will not profit from any sales of the Bolt, it is certainly still moving toward his goal of reducing carbon emissions from driving. On an ideological level, Musk is likely ecstatic that other companies are running with his ideas and using this technology for the eventual good of humanity. Still, the wider availability of electric cars—and the fact that Tesla Motors is no longer the only game in town—will undoubtedly have an impact on both the company's profit margin and his personal financial state.

Chapter 13: Conclusion

Elon Musk's life has been a series of ups and downs. From his complicated childhood through his early business disappointments, the struggles in his personal life, and the shifting nature of his fortune, Musk has shown an implacable determination and dedication to his end goal. It is this dedication that had allowed him to stay the course, even when success seemed nearly impossible. Indeed, doing the impossible has become something of a theme in Musk's life.

Though his investments, fortune, and technological developments have made him an international celebrity, Elon Musk has remained relatively close-mouthed about his personal life. His tumultuous relationship with his second wife, actress Talulah Riley, has spilled over at times into his social media accounts, but he has carefully kept gossip and information about his five children from his first marriage out of the public eye. It is possible this is another trait he acquired from his now-estranged father; even through his oldest son's rise to fame, Errol Musk has chosen to stay out of the limelight, and numerous times has requested that reporters and bloggers not talk about him when they are writing about Elon.

Elon Musk's financial future may be uncertain, but he is on track to achieve his goal of putting human beings on the surface of Mars within his lifetime. For most people to say they plan to colonize the red planet in 20 years would result in skepticism and eye rolling. Indeed, that was the way people reacted when Musk first proposed the concept. In the 15 years of SpaceX's existence to date, Musk has multiple times achieved the impossible.

His spacecraft were the first commercial propulsion-fueled jets to dock with the International Space Station, and the first launch vehicle stages to successfully land on a solid surface, making them the first potentially reusable rockets ever to be made. His innovative approach to plug-in cars through Tesla Motors has made them a viable and legitimate form of transportation that's affordable even for the middle-class. Though people continue to say that Hyperloop technology will never work, the first tests conducted by Hyperloop One seem to prove otherwise.

Reports put out in early 2016 described it as one of Musk's worst years to date, based solely on his financial losses, but if you ask Musk, he may have a different opinion. The first half of 2016 was full of impressive achievements, from the high pre-order demand for Tesla Motors' upcoming Model 3 to the successful vertical landing of their first stage rocketry, from the first tests of his proposed Hyperloop technology to the launch of OpenAI's beta playground. Musk has never put profit ahead of innovation, and however his companies are doing on the stock exchange, there's no denying that each new entry he makes into the record books gets him one step closer to achieving his ultimate dream for humanity.

30 Lesser Known Facts

So we know all the big stuff, where he grew up, what his childhood was like, what drives him and how he arrived at where he is today. But what else is there and what else is there to learn about one of the most mysterious men on Earth. At times it would seem that his life is straight out of science fiction movie and this isn't too far from the truth. In fact, Robert Downey Jr modelled himself on Musk when filming Iron Man. So, of course, it only seemed natural that Musk himself would put in an appearance in Iron Man II. Below, we've compiled some weird and wonderful facts about the real life Iron Man from his favorite video games to how quickly he can eat a hamburger.

1. He hates scripts. When speaking at events, he refuses to rehearse or look at the autocue, preferring to speak off the top of his head. If you've ever seen Elon give a presentation then you'll realize how impressive this really is. With his laid back confidence and effortless speaking manner, it would seem that he's a natural orator.

2. After the sale of Zip2, he purchased a much sought after F1 McLaren as a reward which he then went on to crash.

3. However, he then created the Tesla Model S which is far faster than the Mclaren.

4. He has five children, but just like in every other aspect of his life, only the rare and extraordinary will do. He is the proud father of one set of twins and one set of triplets, an incredibly rare occurrence.

5. He manages his time impeccably with the help of an app. This helps him spread his time evenly amongst his companies. He's known to spend Mondays and Tuesdays at SpaceX, Wednesdays and Thursdays at Tesla and Fridays are split between the both. (Pressman, 2016)

6. He can eat his favorite hamburger in precisely three bites.

7. When he's traveling to Palo Alto, he says he likes to remain "homeless", preferring to stay on friend's couches rather than staying in a hotel. He doesn't see this as a hindrance but instead sees this time as a way to connect with people and brainstorm ideas.

8. Elon is inspired by movies so much that the automated robots at Tesla are named after X Men characters; Xavier, Iceman, Wolverine, Storm, Colossus, Vulcan and Havoc.

9. His mother has been one of the most successful models in the world for over fifty years and is still working today.

10. His dream of colonizing Mars isn't just a fun pipe dream. He genuinely wants to save humanity from certain extinction. He thinks it won't be long until we can no longer rely on planet Earth as our home and that the only way we can survive is to become an interplanetary species.

11. He reads so much that he's remembered large passages from the most technical and complicated books. He is often known to win arguments by citing long passages from them.

12. Just for fun, he constructed a rollercoaster inside the Tesla factory.

13. He loves to put in the occasional cameo role in his favorite shows and once appeared in the Big Bang Theory.

14. At 24 he was all set to pursue his PhD in applied physics but suddenly came down with a case of what he calls FOMO – fear of missing out. His fear was that the internet boom was passing him by so only two days into his PhD, he dropped out and founded Zip2.

15. He has a unique hiring policy, insisting on hiring everybody himself, from assembly line workers to managers. This is no easy task when you remember that SpaceX has 500 employees alone. He also has a "no assholes" policy which means that he only hires people who he thinks are fun and pleasant to be around. He says when someone starts acting like a bit of an asshole they get one warning, if they continue to act like an asshole then they get promptly fired. He cites this as one of the most important elements to hiring his employees saying that if you hate your boss then you're not going to want to come into work and you're not going to work hard. So although skill and experience are important factors in being hired by Musk, one of the most important things you can have is a positive attitude. He also says that he likes to hire people who he sees as having a good heart.

16. He always likes to keep things light-hearted and has placed Easter eggs in the software of all the Tesla cars.

17. After moving to Canada, he had to take on a series of menial jobs to survive. One of these included shovelling dirt in a boiler room.

18. He loves going to Burning Man and once described it as another Silicon Valley. It is also said to be the inspiration behind Solar City.

19. When he was a child he was known to experiment with homemade explosives saying that it's a miracle he made it through to adulthood with all his fingers.

20. He was bullied so severely at school that he once had to be hospitalized after being thrown down the stairs and beaten unconscious. After this, he retreated into the world of technology and sci-fi as a means to escape and it wasn't long until computers took over every aspect of his life.

21. Although Elon never drank alcohol in college, he was known to throw some of the best parties. When he and his best friend found an abandoned twelve bedroom frat house, it was so dilapidated that they got a cut price deal on the rent. After this, they began throwing parties every Saturday night that have since become the stuff of legend. He even charged an admission of $5 dollars and since he was the only sober person in the building, he found it easy to take care of the finances.

22. He was once held at gunpoint in Russia because he attempted to buy 3 $7million rockets. He only managed to escape by bribing the local police.

23. In fact, he hasn't had the best experience of Russia having been spat on by a Russian rocket designer and taunted for not having enough money. However, it was this experience that inspired him to build his own.

24. His five sons have some seriously awesome names; Griffin, Saxon, Kai, Damian and Xavier.

25. His favorite drink these days is whisky.

26. He loves to play video games, especially first person shooters like Bioshock, Fallout, Civilization and Mass Effect.

27. He's the proud owner of an Aero L-39 jet.

28. With his grueling work schedule, it's no surprise that he has a difficult time staying alert. He often consumes around 8 Diet Cokes a day as well as large amounts of coffee.

29. Although he likes to work out twice a week, alternating between running on a treadmill and lifting weight, he admits that he has a terrible diet. He often skips breakfast, eats his lunch in a hurry, usually during meetings and often eats enough for two at dinner. With his favorite food being BBQ and French cuisine.

30.He tries to live his life and make important business decisions by adhering to the first principles of physics.

Top 15 Quotes

We all love a good quote, we can identify with them and read them when we need to be emotionally lifted. They can keep us motivated while inspiring us and letting us know that we're not alone. Elon is a master of the inspirational quote and doesn't hold back. You'll often find him at SpaceX saying what, on the surface, seems the craziest thing. However, even his most weird and wonderful quotes show just how much of a genius he is and how he's never far away from a brand new wacky idea. It makes us wonder if Elon has ever had a normal, boring thought in his life.

1. While discussing whether humans are the product of someone else's video game he said:

"I've had so many simulation discussions it's crazy. In fact, it got to the point where basically every conversation was the AI-slash-simulation conversation, and my brother and I finally agreed that we'd ban any such conversations if we're ever in a hot tub. Because that really kills the magic." (Wile, 2010)

2. If you've ever trawled through the immense amount of internet data on Elon, then chances are you will at some point reach a bizarre and perplexing conspiracy theory that he's actually a Martian. It's completely crazy and unfounded but apparently there are thousands of people in the world who believe that he has somehow been trapped on Earth. That' why he's trying to build a spaceship to make it back to his home planet. This is mainly because of his sheer determination to get to Mars but also because his intellect and scope of achievement almost seems other worldly. In a series of tweets on the 12th of March, 2015, he has this to say:

"Seems like an opportune moment to bring up the Fermi Paradox, aka 'where are the aliens?' Really odd that we see no sign of them. Btw, please don't mention the pyramids. Stacking stone blocks is not evidence of an advanced civilization. The rumor that I'm building a spaceship to get back to my home planet Mars is totally untrue. The ancient Egyptians were amazing, but if aliens built the pyramids, they would've left behind a computer or something."

3. As mentioned previously, he has a somewhat rocky relationship with the Russians. This quote comes from his book, *Elon Musk: Tesla, Space X, and the Quest for a Fantastic Future.*

"My family fears that the Russians will assassinate me."

4. It's not too unusual to see offices around Silicon Valley with quirky interior design and a playful environment. Of course, Elon wanted to do something far more extravagant.

"Everybody around here has slides in their lobbies. I'm actually wondering about putting in a roller coaster — like a functional roller coaster at the factory in Fremont. You'd get in, and it would take you around [the] factory but also up and down. Who else has a roller coaster? … It would probably be really expensive, but I like the idea of it." (Floersch, 2015)

5. Have you ever wondered why we've almost reached the third decade of the millennium but we still don't have flying cars? This is what Elon had to say to Business Insider about them:

"I've thought about it quite a lot … We could definitely make a flying car – but that's not the hard part … The hard part is, how do you make a flying car that's super safe and quiet? Because if it's a howler, you're going to make people very unhappy." (Wile, 2010)

6. You would think that the most technological instruments to ever exist would have a patent but Elon doesn't believe in them. He told Wired about a mission to mars:

"We have essentially no patents in SpaceX. Our primary long-term competition is in China — if we published patents, it would be farcical, because the Chinese would just use them as a recipe book." (Anderson, 2012)

7. At one of his birthday parties he was asked to hold a balloon between his legs while someone attempted to pop it by throwing a knife at it. Although terrifying for most people, Elon says:

"I'd seen him before but did worry that maybe he could have an off day. Still, I thought, he would maybe hit one gonad but not both."

8. When Ford decided he wasn't allowed to use the letter 'E' in one of his car's names, he wasn't best pleased. And instead of doing as he was told, he told Ford exactly what he thought:

"Like why did you go steal Tesla's E? Like you're some sort of fascist army marching across the alphabet, some sort of Sesame Street robber?" (Muoio, 2016)

9. Despite manufacturing cars, he actually doesn't have a particularly positive outlook on the things.

"In the distant future, people may outlaw driving cars because it's too dangerous. You can't have a person driving a two-ton death machine."

10. While thinking about how he'd like to die, he says:

"I would like to die on Mars. Just not on impact."

11. When talking about bringing things to fruition from its conception:

"(Physics is) a good framework for thinking. ... Boil things down to their fundamental truths and reason up from there."

12. We've seen before that he's not the type of person to give up. And again he says:

"Persistence is very important. You should not give up unless you are forced to give up." (Kim, 2016)

13. Aside from making sure not to hire assholes, he has some other ideas on sourcing the best staff.

"It is a mistake to hire huge numbers of people to get a complicated job done. Numbers will never compensate for talent in getting the right answer (two people who don't know something are no better than one), will tend to slow down progress, and will make the task incredibly expensive." (Kim, 2016)

14. We all know that Mars is freezing and an unlikely place where humans would want to inhabit. When asked about how we could make the red, dusty planet more hospitable, he had a pretty simple answer:

"The fast way is to drop thermonuclear weapons over the poles."

15. Although he's certain we do live inside a simulation, he of course understands there's a chance we do not. On the off chance we're not simulated consciousness swimming around someone's vision of a programmed civilization, he says:

"Arguably we should hope that that's true, because otherwise if civilization stops advancing, that may be due to some calamitous event that erases civilization. So maybe we should be hopeful that this is a simulation, because otherwise...

We are either going to create simulations indistinguishable from reality or civilization ceases to exist." (New God Argument)

Thank You

I hope you enjoyed the book. Can I please ask you a favor? Would you be so kind to leave a review on Amazon? It really helps to keep me going and write more about amazing people like Elon.

Bibliography

Anderson, C. (2012, October 21). *Elon Musk's Mission to Mars*. Retrieved February 20, 2017, from Wired: https://www.wired.com/2012/10/ff-elon-musk-qa/all/

Cappuccino, J. (2016, August 27). *Is this Tech Billionaire Trying to Date Amber Heard After Her Divorce?* Retrieved February 20, 2017, from Elite Daily: http://elitedaily.com/entertainment/celebrity/amber-heard-elon-musk-dating-after-divorce/1593845/

Floersch, A. (2015, May 14). *Top 8 Elon Musk Quotes: The Muskinator*. Retrieved February 20, 2017, from Areavoices: https://alexandrafloersch.areavoices.com/top-8-elon-musk-quotes-the-muskinator/

Greenfield, L. (2010, SEptember 10). *"I Was a Starter Wife": Inside America's Messiest Divorce*. Retrieved February 20, 2017, from Marie Claire: http://www.marieclaire.com/sex-love/advice/a5380/millionaire-starter-wife/

Kim, L. (2016, March 8). *50 Innovation and Success Quotes from SpaceX Founder Elon Musk*. Retrieved February 20, 2017, from Inc.: http://www.inc.com/larry-kim/50-innovation-amp;-success-quotes-from-spacex-founder-elon-musk.html

Muoio, D. (2016, November 16). *6 Lesser-Know Secrets About Tesla Cars*. Retrieved February 20, 2017, from Business Insider: http://tech.economictimes.indiatimes.com/news/technology/6-lesser-known-secrets-about-tesla-cars/55449894

New God Argument. (n.d.). *Technologists on the Simulation Hypothesis*. Retrieved February 20, 2017, from

The New God Argument: https://new-god-argument.com/support/technologists-simulation-hypothesis.html

Pressman, M. (2016, May 3). *Little Known Facts About Tesla CEO Elon Musk*. Retrieved February 20, 2017, from Evannex: https://evannex.com/blogs/news/116268037-little-known-facts-about-tesla-ceo-elon-musk-free-ebook

Pritzker, P. (2014, March 31). *The New 'Economic Census' Will Help Unleash teh Economic Magic of the U.S. Government Data*. Retrieved February 20, 2017, from Forbes: http://www.forbes.com/sites/realspin/2014/03/28/the-new-economic-census-will-help-unleash-the-economic-magic-of-u-s-government-data/#174f629c67fa

Shandrow, K. L. (2016, September 23). *5 Out of This World Songs That Inspire Elon Musk*. Retrieved February 20, 2017, from Entrepreneur: https://www.entrepreneur.com/article/282804

Silver, R. (n.d.). *10 Best Books on Becoming a Millionaire in Business*. Retrieved Febraury 20, 2017, from Everyday Power : http://everydaypowerblog.com/2016/06/25/books-on-becoming-a-millionaire/

Wile, R. (2010, July 8). *Elon Musk: Correcting the Record About My Divorce*. Retrieved February 20, 2017, from Business Insider: http://www.businessinsider.com/correcting-the-record-about-my-divorce-2010-7

Printed in Great Britain
by Amazon